PRESENTING FOR
WOMEN IN BUSINESS

PRESENTING FOR WOMEN IN BUSINESS

Carole McKenzie

MERCURY

Copyright © Carole McKenzie 1991

All rights reserved. No part of this publication may be reproduced, stored in a retrieval system, or transmitted in any form or by any means, electronic, mechanical, photocopying, recording, or otherwise without the prior permission of the publishers.

First published in 1991
by Mercury Books
Gold Arrow Publications Limited,
862 Garratt Lane, London SW17 0NB

Set in Melior by TecSet Limited
Printed and bound in Great Britain by
Mackays of Chatham plc, Chatham, Kent

This book is sold subject to the condition that it shall not, by way of trade or otherwise, be lent, re-sold, hired out or otherwise circulated without the publisher's prior consent in any form of binding or cover other than that in which it is published and without a similar condition including this condition being imposed upon the subsequent purchaser.

British Library Cataloguing in Publication Data

McKenzie, Carole
 Presenting for women in business.
 I. Title
 808.5082
 ISBN 1-85251-140-0

Contents

Preface		vii
Acknowledgements		ix
1	The Demographics	1
2	Initial Preparation	17
3	Structure	31
4	Putting Your Notes Together	45
5	Communication	63
6	Body Language	75
7	Visual Aids	97
8	Questions	117
9	Set up and Rehearsal	131
10	Other Types of Presentation	135
11	Survey	147
12	The Secrets of Effective Women Presenters	173

Contents

13	What Men Look For in Women Presenters	187
14	The Future	199
Bibliography		203
Index		205

Preface

According to a recent survey, speaking in public ranks second to rats, but beats death into third place on most people's dread list. So many do need help. And the shelves are full of 'teach yourself' books. So what makes this book different?

There is a widely-held view that it is more difficult for women to be effective presenters, particularly when dealing with male audiences. Furthermore, few women have access to the secrets of the female role models in this field. *Presenting For Women in Business* covers these points in detail and shares with you the views of women in business. In particular, this book features: attitudes towards the subject; feelings about giving presentations; presenters most admired and why; and key success factors. It also contains advice from well-known names in business, the media and politics; and it reveals what men think about women presenters.

Presenting For Women in Business will do more than improve your presentation skills. If you are a new manager, an experienced manager, or one of the countless women who will be called upon to speak in public for the first time, take heart and learn from successful women presenters.

The number of public speaking opportunities has greatly increased over the last few years and the demand will continue to grow in the 1990s. Today men and women need to respond to this growing demand. Privatisation and corporate restructuring mean that more share-

Preface

holders want a say at their AGM. More parents want to determine how their children's schools are run. More people are becoming interested in community affairs, environmental issues and joining pressure groups. Managers at all levels are now expected to speak at meetings and conferences. As more and more women join the workforce and climb the career ladder or join networking and social groups, the prospects of avoiding the challenge of making presentations are now very small.

Finally, anyone who witnessed Margaret Thatcher's last performance as Prime Minister at Question Time in the House cannot fail to have been impressed, regardless of their politics, or forget her comment, 'I'm enjoying this!' as she skilfully fielded questions from the floor. I hope that those words will ring true for you when next you stand up to speak in public!

Carole McKenzie
June 1991

Acknowledgements

The ideas in this book have been developed over several years. I am indebted to the many hundreds of men and women who have attended my courses and added to my knowledge and enjoyment of the subject.

I would particularly like to thank the many people in business, politics and the media who have given generously of their advice. Thanks also to the members of Women in Management who responded to the survey.

I would also like to thank my husband, John, and son Scot, for their never-ending love and support.

'I gather your wife has returned to work, Mr Smith.'

1
The Demographics

> 'Let the great world spin for ever down the ringing grooves of change.'
> *Alfred, Lord Tennyson*

IMPLICATIONS FOR CHANGE IN THE 1990s

The demographic time bomb which is hitting Britain in the 1990s will encourage more women to seek employment and force more companies to offer real equality. The position of women in society is changing. Attitudes are shifting and change is the only certainty for the future of women and work.

More than a century ago Thomas Campbell wrote: 'Coming events cast their shadow before them.' This has never been more true. Many employers are aware that more attention needs to be given to attracting and developing women. They are also aware that failing to do so will mean that they will be outpaced by their competitors in the race to gain the skilled workforce they need.

This book owes its origins to two factors: first, concern about the effects of this impending demographic timebomb and the impact it will have on both men and women; and second, my own growing awareness that many women are not particularly good at blowing their own trumpets – even when they are capable of great music.

What does the demographic timebomb mean for women? The Vision for the 1990s, as set out in a Government White Paper, describes three fundamental influences on employment and training:

- demography
- global competition
- changing nature of employment

The impact of demographic change, inadequate past training and skills shortages is clear. Employers now need to turn to alternative sources of labour, including women returners, and stop treating women as second-class workers. Company policies, including the training policy, need to be broadened to accommodate women with family responsibilities. The Government backs up this statement with the following statistical predictions:

- The number of under 25s in the labour market will fall by 1.2 million between 1989 and 1995.
- 80 per cent of the labour force in the year 2000 will be made up of people already in the labour force.
- By 1995 there will be an increase of 750,000 married women in the labour force (80 per cent of the total increase).

The EOC (Equal Opportunities Commission) responded to this paper with strategies for action which would remove barriers to women's participation. These barriers include:

- inadequate child care provision
- restrictive job and training requirements
- inflexible working terms and conditions.

The Demographics

Quality, not just quantity, of jobs for women will be the key issue for the Commission in the 1990s. Action is needed now to address these issues. Virtually all the projected growth will result from women taking a more active role in the labour market. Women are expected to make up 45 per cent of the labour force by 2001!

It is clear from these figures and also from the response of the EOC and other organisations that the issue is being taken seriously. John Rigg of the Henley Centre maintains that the companies that will prosper in the 1990s are those planning *now* for the reduction in the numbers of young people and already looking at alternative sources of employees. (The demographic changes also mean that employers are aware of the changes in the number of young people available for employment.) This has led to a few leading companies encouraging older women into the workforce. During the 1980s older people were encouraged to take early retirement; but in the mid 1990s, with an ageing population and fewer young people available for work, employers will have to encourage more flexible retirement practices.

The Under-Utilisation of Women in the Labour Market Report states that more than a million women do not return to work after having children because of poor childcare provision, low pay and lack of part-time work. Employers could ease the problem of declining numbers of young people by appealing to this alternative source. Currently, over half a million women are not working because childcare costs too much or is not available. Midland Bank is the best known example of an employer attempting childcare provision, with its planned national network of workplace nurseries.

The Report also found that of the declining numbers of unemployed upon whom employers can draw to fill the gaps in the job market, ethnic minorities and the disabled make up a disproportionate number. So employers can shield themselves from the effects of demographic change by exploring ways of attracting alternative sources of labour. Thus change is an opportunity, as well as a threat!

> **'Change is not made without inconvenience, even from worse to better.'**
>
> *Anon.*

These wise words were spoken by a seventeenth century theologian. Change is very often a slow process and new processes and attitudes are not adopted overnight. Despite the fact that employers are aware of the impending timebomb, many are slow to accommodate change. Some companies congratulate themselves on promoting women into higher positions up to a certain point, which women have dubbed the glass ceiling. They achieve a certain level, can see where they want to go, but some barrier prevents further progress.

Men and women have different qualities to offer. Most modern women don't want to be like men; often they try, don't like it and refuse to compete further. Many women speak of being 'honorary men'. I recently watched a television programme featuring women's issues in the 1990s. Angela Rumbold, MP answered questions from the audience. One woman expressed the view that for women to be listened to they had to be aggressive. Angela Rumbold replied, 'We don't need to be aggressive – we just need to be good'. She also challenged the questioners who thought that little had been achieved in the 1980s to promote women's issues, responding with the comment that having a woman Prime Minister has put paid to the suggestion that women can't make it to the top. Few people would argue with this view, but many women would welcome career progression without the feeling that they have to give up some of their femininity; and the freedom to admit their mistakes and not feel vulnerable. It is interesting that Ronald Reagan described Margaret Thatcher as 'the best man in England'.

There is still much to be done and attitudes are changing only slowly. What is clear is that women

The Demographics

acknowledge that they have a choice. They can say 'yes' or 'no' to marriage, children, a career – indeed, they may choose all three. Whatever choice is made, support mechanisms need to be in place to endorse their decision.

Women who have made the choice feel that the attitudes of men are a stumbling block to career advancement. Recent research reported in the *Sunday Times* revealed that the fact that men outnumber women at middle, senior and board level in all the companies studied made women feel inferior. In the words of one graduate in her twenties, 'It's bloody hard work being a woman manager. You have to fight all the way and really prove yourself to get anywhere. The first woman at board level in this company would be the eighth wonder of the world.'

Many women managers feel that a lack of female role models at middle and senior management levels could discourage women from joining the company, or from making long-term career plans. They also feel that women are not treated equally, often blaming men for their failure to get to the top. This was revealed in recent survey results on leadership training. Both sexes blame the attitudes of their colleagues. It was found that 60 per cent of personnel and training managers see male acceptance as the biggest challenge to women as leaders. Confidence is cited as the second.

Women manufacturing managers are few and far between. Picture the scene: a noisy, car-manufacturing production line. Above it there is the cacophony of conveyors, air tools and Tina Turner. Blasting out from the trackside comes a series of piercing wolf whistles together with the thumping of spanners on metal . . .

This is a typical experience of a woman manager on her daily walk through the factory and one which, if roles were reversed, would make the majority of males feel very uncomfortable. So why do some men exhibit this type of behaviour? Are they trying to warn us that this is their environment and that we are trespassing? Whatever the reason, this sort of attitude towards women is not limited to the motor industry. It is far more widespread and may be one reason why there are still so few women managers.

Bronwen Curtis, vice-president of manufacturing for Avon Cosmetics, is no feminist. She has never pushed herself as a woman or deliberately set out to succeed in a man's world.

'I've always tried to be a good manager', she states. 'I honestly believe I've got here on merit – not because I'm a woman. Men and women are different; they have different strengths and weaknesses. Yet some women try to prove they are equal when they are not. They should stop worrying about being women and concentrate on being good managers.' Reinforcing this view, Bronwen says she was paid the ultimate compliment when her appointment as Avon's first female director was announced. A manager phoned to congratulate her, saying, 'I've never really thought of you as a woman!'. Some would have been offended; she was delighted.

According to *Female Resource*, a journal for women managers, the last thirteen years have seen women double their share of management positions. In 1975 11 per cent of all employees in management positions were women; by 1988 this had increased to 20 per cent. Unfortunately, these figures are not reflected throughout the manufacturing industry. For example, a large automotive manufacturer in February 1990 still had only 2.4 per cent of its 2,042 management positions occupied by women.

Sheila Browning is a director of a Dundee consultancy and training organisation. Despite an impressive array of qualifications, Sheila feels that she has to be significantly better at her job than her male counterparts, a comment which emerges regularly in conversations with women managers. She believes it's because women in industry (even those with exactly the same qualifications as their male colleagues) are still not accepted as equals. 'It's all

The Demographics

about assumptions', she says. 'People assume men are capable of doing a job, whereas women have to prove they can do it.' She believes that women are less inclined to plan their careers or have a career development strategy, but feels that the demographic trends will help. Companies will have to treat women better, give them accountability and a sense of ownership.

Director and customer services manager at Vishay-Mann, Linda Steel, recalls the time she attended a day-long seminar hosted by one of the learned engineering institutions. Linda Steel was a novelty. She received special attention – until, that is, she asked for the women's room! Confusion reigned. No one knew where it was, or if, indeed, it existed. Eventually she was ushered up several flights of stairs to use the staff facilities.

That was several years ago. Manufacturing management was dominated by men, many of whom aimed to keep it that way. However, Linda Steel believes that the climate has changed since then. She feels that men are accepting female managers, and that it is women's fault there are so few. A self-confessed workaholic, Linda displays a commitment she feels is sometimes lacking in other managers. However, she stresses that this has nothing to do with gender:

'Good managers have qualities which make them good. For example, they deal well with people, they listen, they're decisive and they're committed to improving their companies. When it comes to possessing these qualities, I don't believe you can distinguish between men and women – it's all about individuals and who is best for the job.'

Linda doesn't believe in role models. She believes that 'it's what women want to do for themselves. If they've got enough determination, are prepared to push for promotion and take a few knocks, they'll get there.' If that learned engineering institution is anything to go by, industry is getting there too. On a recent visit she found lavatories for the female visitors. One small step . . .

Presenting For Women in Business

Ask Sally-Anne Tsangarides whether she believes women have any particular managerial qualities to bring to manufacturing and she'll reel off a long list. As project and planning manager at Merck, Sharp & Dohme, she is responsible for a team of ten people. Clearly her company actively cultivates equal opportunities for men and women; in a total manufacturing site workforce of 250, there are several female managers, plus many female personnel. Sally-Anne believes women have positive qualities that men lack. Whereas men tend to be task-orientated, women will balance the task and the individual better. She finds the assumptions made about women at work irritating. A lot of companies, she says, still don't expect women to be career-minded and as a result, they don't offer the same amount of training or development opportunities. Industry must be prepared to recruit more women and expose them to the same amount of training as men. And her final plea: don't assume that when a woman answers the phone, she must be the manager's secretary!

The political arena is another area dominated by men. Women who make it into politics must be confident and competent. Edwina Currie believes that the necessary skills must come from standing up in a roomful of horribly hostile men, or before an uncommitted mixed audience (often referred to as UNA = universal non-committed audience); being confident and competent to answer all their questions, complete with the usual digs and asides – and win them over. There is no quarter in politics. She adds, 'Stand up to speak in the House of Commons and both sides will be waiting for the first slip. Tories will imitate a high squeaky voice; Labour men – chauvinists all – will utter ribald comments about hormones. The trick of it all is to take no notice'. Edwina Currie reflects what many women have expressed – that a lot of men aren't very good at politics (this could be any area), but the difference is that they tend to try and we women tend to give up.

The Demographics

Prime Minister John Major's failure to promote more women to the Cabinet reinforces the widespread unease that exists about the predominant maleness of public life. When Margaret Thatcher came to power over a decade ago, there were only another eighteen women MPs. By 1990 this figure had more than doubled, although women MPs are still outnumbered by fourteen to one. This stems from the fact that vastly more male than female candidates have been putting themselves forward for selection. The good news is that many more women are now coming forward and equality is not so much an issue.

At the end of 1990 statistics from the Labour Force Survey showed that one of the most substantial rises in women's participation was in the area of self-employment. There were 750,000 working-age women in self-employment in 1989, i.e. more than double the figure of 272,000 at the end of the previous decade. Women have come a long way in the 1980s, but there is still a long way to go. The 1990s will provide women with new opportunities and challenges. This is not to say that women's hitherto slippery ascent to the corporate pinnacles is suddenly going to become easy. Nor will it be easy for men; they will have to rethink long-established attitudes and assumptions about what women want, and what they are capable of contributing. The successful companies in the 1990s will be those who employ the best talent available, irrespective of gender.

Organisations such as the EOC are continuing to work to bring about change through equal opportunity. Many women MPs from all Parties are speaking out for women's issues. Rosie Barnes, MP and many others feel that they have a responsibility to take them up. She believes there aren't enough women's voices to represent the daily issues in women's lives.

At the beginning of the last decade a hundred women's organisations in Britain, representing two million members, came together under the title 'Women's Action'. They agreed on eight points of direct concern to the majority of women which they felt demanded Parliamentary action during the 1980s. Last year, a half of *one* of these points (individual taxation for everyone) – achieved statutory success. The other seven and a half are still awaiting Parliamentary action.

Lady Howe, wife of the former Deputy Prime Minister, speaking on the Report on Women at the Top (published recently by the Hansard Society Commission) admits that 'the proportion of women MPs is wholly unacceptable in a modern democracy.' She describes the report as 'frankly, just one more drip on the stone of what is happening and what needs to be done.'

FUTURE OPTIMISM

> **'The only way out is through.'**
> *Helen Keller*

Does the glass ceiling exist? Many women think that it is more imaginary than real. Angela Rumbold, MP believes that she has been through it and in one of the most difficult of all zones, the political one. She feels that, ultimately, the final push will come from women who themselves will want to take the opportunities on offer. Women should be prepared to widen their career horizons. They must also be prepared to work to obtain the necessary skills and qualifications. If you want to succeed, the most important lesson in life is that you must want to succeed badly enough to make it a reality.

Detta O'Cathain, managing director of the Barbican Centre, believes that 'shattering the glass ceiling' is a very aggressive term, with its implications of destruction and violence. In a presentation to Women in Management, Detta invented a new way of expressing it. She turned to Lewis Carroll's *Alice Through the Looking Glass* and noted Alice saying, 'Let's pretend the glass has gone all

The Demographics

soft like gauze, so we can get through'. Is Lewis Carroll saying to women, 'Think positively and you'll get there'? Getting through takes confidence; lack of confidence, inadequate training, attitudes of male colleagues, insufficient role models, these are seen by many women to be the main reasons for women's lack of progress.

A well-known television presenter, when asked why more high-flying women did not appear on his programme, stated that 'Such people are hard to find.' Carole Stone, the former producer of Radio 4's *Any Questions*, admits that what interests more and more listeners is hearing informed views from people who are actually *doing* things, the experts in their own fields. The problem is that people who can communicate pithily, engagingly and with touches of humour are quite thin on the ground. She believes that women are more likely to let any lack of self-confidence show; BBC producers say that women admit too freely to knowing nothing about some subjects, whereas men in the same position would never knowingly undermine themselves. The only way to become a seasoned performer is through practice, and women have a lot of catching up to do.

Many women report that they are afraid to take that first step, to express their views or seek promotion. Others believe that if you confront areas of anxiety and move through the anxiety, creating experiences rather than circling them, you will have something to show for it. The fear disappears and a new confidence emerges. Sheila Browning contends that women are too honest for their own good. Ask a man whether he is capable of doing a job and he'll say 'yes' whether or not he can really cope. Ask a woman and, if she's not sure, she'll say so.

The NEDO report on 'Women Managers: the Untapped Resource', reveals that only 1 per cent of top management are women, only 4 per cent in senior and middle management, and that overall there are only 27 per cent. One thing is clear – change is inevitable. There are many role models in business, the media and politics, who are articulate and successful. Maybe we, as women, are not listening and learning from them. What does come across time after time, when they are asked why they are successful, is this: by combining ability with sensitivity, integrity and hard work, women can succeed in a male-dominated world. Women don't need to compete in the 'better than' men circuit, but on equal terms.

Women possess innate qualities which equip them well for management in this decade. We are trained from an early age to multi-task, employ time management techniques, and we are adept at getting the best out of people. We have qualities which are different from those of men. We need to acknowledge the differences and work at building up our self-confidence. Many successful women feel that acceptance of their own abilities is the first step towards male acceptance. This is summed up nicely in the quotation: 'If I am not for myself, who will be for me? If I am only for myself, who am I?'

As women become more involved in management, the corporate philosophy will have to change in order to bring their working lives on a par with those of their male counterparts, says Frederica Olivares, CEO of Olivares Edizioni Publishing Company. If one word could explain the decade leading up to the year 2000, it is globalisation. Frederica believes that this is also true for women in management in Western societies and economies. Why? Not only because business and professional opportunities are rapidly going global in terms of dimensions and markets, but also because the cultural environment is turning into a global village. Values, attitudes and life-styles are integrating so rapidly throughout Europe that all positive and negative events affect the opportunities and the image of women in management and leave an impact on the issue as a whole. Consequently, the future of women in management will undoubtedly be more homogeneous and linked on a European and international basis.

The Demographics

European countries have produced undeniable talent, competence and successful performances in a wide and unfamiliar range of business fields. Therefore, a number of role models have emerged and permeated the minds, aspirations and choices of younger generations of women. Also, it has to be considered that new market challenges and integrations (such as 1992) stir up nations and companies to strive for a comparable level of social innovation. A higher percentage of women managers has already been considered a competitive advantage. Managing globally calls for an array of skills.

Yet there are less than 3 per cent of women in international management. They represent a resource impossible to overlook. Why? Because women are traditionally stronger in those skills requiring greater cross-cultural sophistication. These are skills that many fast-track managers lack, such as the patience for relationship development, communication and social sensitivity across cultural differences. The challenge for companies in the future is to provide flexibility and a range of options, so that both men and women can raise their families as they see fit and still contribute. The challenge for men and women in management is to make our organisations not only better places to work in, but also better places to live in.

Meanwhile, women need to believe in their abilities and talents and think positively. If, for example, you are the only woman among ten interviewees, or the only one speaking at a conference, that's a bonus – you get remembered. You want to be remembered for the right reasons, and communication skills is one of the management training areas which many women feel will assist them in getting their views known. Many organisations and employers have introduced innovative training and re-training schemes to fill this need and this book will help you to improve your presentation skills. If you are a new manager, an experienced manager, or one of the countless women who will be called upon to speak in public for the first time, take heart, and useful advice, from women who have already done it.

The number of public speaking opportunities has greatly increased over the last few years and the demand will continue to grow in the 1990s. Today men and women are becoming more involved. Privatisation means that more shareholders want a say at their AGM. More parents want to determine how their children's schools are run. People are becoming interested in community affairs, environmental issues and pressure groups. Managers at all levels are now expected to speak at meetings and conferences. As more and more women enter the workforce and climb the career ladder, join networking and social groups, the chances of escaping the challenge of presentations is now very small. Maybe there will come a time when you actually welcome and enjoy giving presentations.

Finally, Tom Peters, co-author of the management classic *In Search of Excellence*, has a new principle: 'women first'. He believes that the best new managers will listen, motivate and support. Isn't that just like a woman?

National Alliance of Women's Organisations (NAWO) Survey:

What women wanted in 1980

- Index-linked child benefits
- flexible working hours
- crèches, after school and holiday care
- equal pay for work of equal value and individual taxation
- same retirement age for men and women

The Demographics

- equal educational opportunities for girls and boys
- representative groups of women on housing, town planning and environmental committees
- maternity, gynaecological and family planning services that meet the real needs of women.

What women want in 1990

- recognition of women's true role in the economy
- environmental policies to allow for women's needs
- education and training
- increased support for families and for carers
- preventive health care
- equal representation of women in public life
- cooperation among women internationally
- undistorted images of women in media
- to be protected against violence, both in society and at home
- independent access to housing.

2
Initial Preparation

'Nothing will ever be attempted if all possible objections must first be overcome.'
Dr Samuel Johnson

When asked what they find most difficult when preparing a presentation, many women say it is getting started. Some of the excuses given are: insufficient time to plan, false starts, mental blocks, and general lack of motivation. Usually this frustration will be caused by one of the following:

- **It's your first time!**
  If you have little or no experience in giving presentations, this book will take you step by step through the different stages. Read the chapters on preparation, structure and notes, and then attempt to put your presentation together. Invite a colleague to sit in on your practice and ask him or her to give you some constructive feedback. If possible, choose someone who is an experienced presenter, and knows something about the presentation topic. He or she can then advise on company style, and suitable visuals.

- **Lack of facts**
  If you are not sure that you have all the facts, you naturally hesitate to prepare your presentation. Do some more research and see if it helps to get you started. To help you in future presentations, create a

fact file. Photocopy research information, newspaper clippings, journal articles. File them under their respective headings. Next time you are asked to give a presentation you will have a useful resource at your disposal.

- **Tunnel vision**

  Perhaps you are so close to the subject that you can't get a good perspective on it. Get some input from other people; whether they have any good ideas or nor, merely explaining the situation to them will often clarify your own thinking.
  Construct a mind map. Often, jotting down the central theme and some key words will open up areas for further exploration.

- **Lack of conviction**

  Maybe you are finding it impossible to get started because, deep down, you don't believe in the value of the exercise or the way in which you've been asked to present it. Instead of procrastinating, face the facts squarely, analyse the pros and cons, and make recommendations for a different course of action. If this is unsuccessful and you must go ahead, remember that your audience should not be aware of any difficulties or disagreements behind the scenes. Be positive and don't let negative feelings or attitudes show.

- **Lack of starting point**

  Often the task seems so daunting that you simply can't figure out how to get started. Use the salami technique, i.e. break it up into manageable areas. It can seem a daunting task when you consider the work involved in putting together a presentation. The preparation checklist will help you. For example, if your presentation is not imminent, you could ease yourself into it by perhaps starting to work on the objectives or

Initial Preparation

the audience profile. By working at it, small steps at a time, the preparation will soon be complete.

- **Fatigue**
  Creative thinking is needed to make effective presentations. This cannot be forced. If you are working on the preparation and are getting nowhere, your best bet is to put it on the back burner overnight and let your subconscious mind take over. Often the solution will come when you least expect it. Work when you are at your best; if you work best in the morning, try to have some preparation time then. Also, if you must prepare at your workplace, ensure that you are not disturbed.

The Chinese have a saying that a journey of a thousand miles begins with a single step. So, too, all undertakings, no matter how large, are comprised of component parts that can usually be tackled one at a time.

Preparing to give presentations can be tackled in this way:

PREPARATION AND PLANNING

You are probably familiar with the saying, 'A well prepared talk is nine-tenths delivered'. My particular favourite is '90 per cent preparation, 10 per cent perspiration'. Very true!

One of the first questions you might ask yourself is, what are your objectives for giving this presentation. In Britain we say, 'What shall we do?' and then, 'I wonder if it will achieve anything?' In America they ask; '*What* do we want to achieve?' and then, '*How* can we achieve it?'

Objectives

What are you trying to achieve? Are you attempting to inform, persuade, motivate, cause them to act, give bad or

Presenting For Women in Business

Preparation and planning

Initial Preparation

good news, discipline, entertain the audience? Decide exactly what the objective(s) is/are.

For example, your objective may be:

- to inform employees of the new benefits package
- to persuade management to implement an electronic mailing system.
- to motivate staff to improve customer service
- to provide an understanding of the potential benefits of establishing a company ethics code.

Try to state your objective in a sentence. Write it on a card and place it in front of you as you prepare. Check that your objectives are **SMART**:

Specific – clear and unambiguous
Measurable – how will you know you have achieved them?
Audience related – should address audience needs
Realistic – able to be achieved
Time – can be done in the time available.

You want to effect change in the audience. What do you want them going away knowing, believing, feeling, doing differently?

AUDIENCE

Who are these people who will attend the presentation? The following checklist will provide a useful audience profile.

Audience Profile

Who do they represent (company, organisation)?
What are their: job titles, responsibilities, backgrounds, levels of knowledge, education, ages?

Presenting For Women in Business

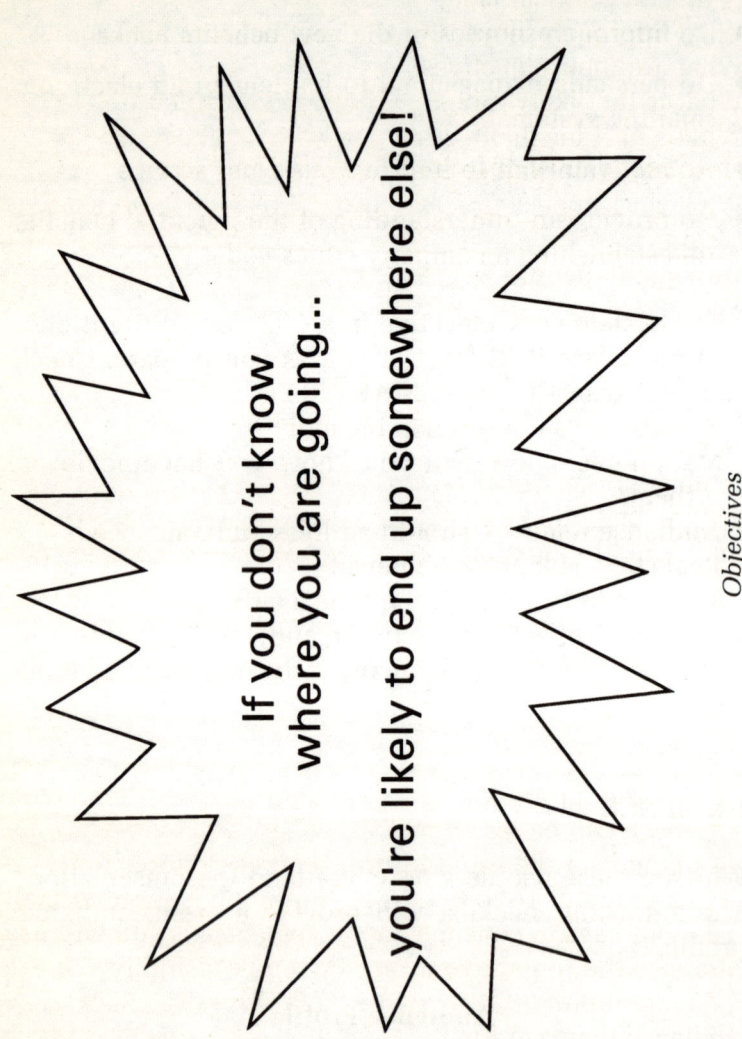

Objectives

Initial Preparation

Is it a mixed audience or all male/female?
Is it a racially mixed audience?
How technical will the presentation be?
Is there a political factor involved?
What approach should I take, informal/formal?
What are their objectives?
What is the likely mood, receptive or hostile?
What's in it for them, i.e. what's the hook?
How important is the presentation to decision making?
What do I expect from them in the way of response or action?
How many people will attend?
Other

The more you can find out about your audience, the better your preparation. Depending on the type of presentation you give, some of the above questions may not be relevant, others may need to be added.

Now that you know *who* is attending the presentation, and *why*, the next step is to decide *where* the audience will sit. In business presentations we are not always consulted about venue and room layout, but here are some guidelines.

Audience size and room layout

In a small group of between 5 and 10 people, your approach can be less formal. You can stand closer to the group and set the room up to encourage interaction.

In a group of 10 to 30, the presentation is more formal. You will have to consider the type of visuals you will use and also the room layout for maximum visibility.

In a group of 30 to 100, the group becomes more of an audience than a group of individuals. The presentation is more formal. Visual aids need to be well designed and projected.

Over 100 in your audience and the event becomes almost a theatrical event. Good lighting and sound are

Presenting For Women in Business

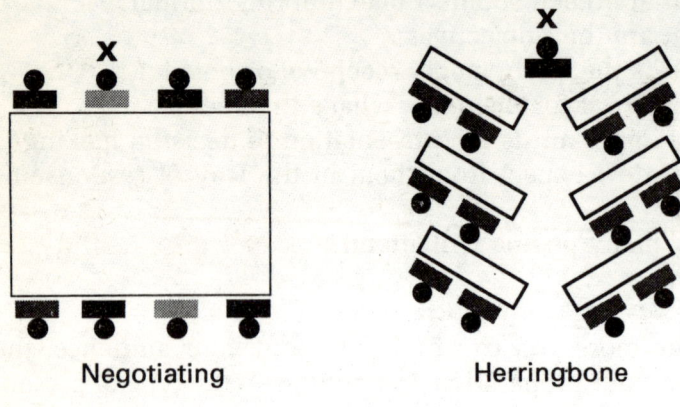

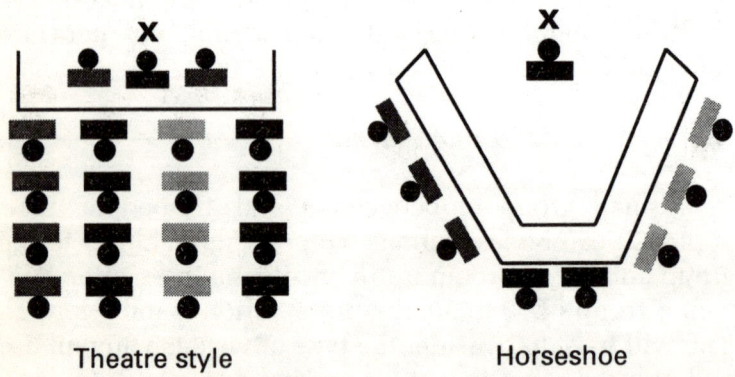

Different room layouts for audience participation

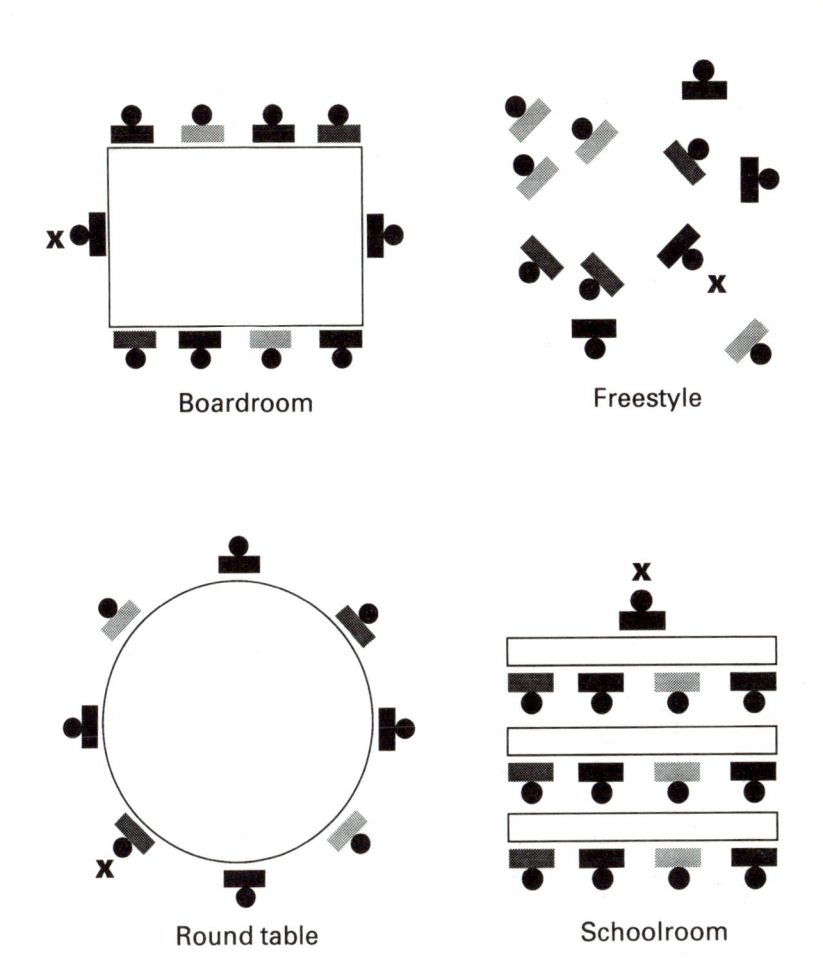

Initial Preparation

Boardroom

Freestyle

Round table

Schoolroom

crucial. Particular care will also be needed to hook and keep audience attention.

There are no hard and fast rules about room layout, except that the audience *must* be able to:

- see and hear the presenter and the visual aids clearly.

- be comfortable for the length of time they will be sitting. For example, check that the room is the correct temperature and if a large group, that it is big enough for the size of audience; similarly, if it is a small group, that the room is not too large.

- communicate – a small audience scattered around a large room makes communication more difficult. In this case, ask the group to come down to the front two or three rows.

Alternative approach

Let us consider what to do if you have insufficient time/information to produce an audience profile.

Often refreshments are served before the presentation begins. In this case, use the time to speak to as many people as possible. Ask a few questions and try to remember some names. That way you are not going in cold.

If it's a very large group, often people register as they arrive. Usually this information will include the name, position and company of each delegate. This basic information is clearly better than none.

Start the presentation by asking a few questions about the audience. For example:

- How many people have used the XYZ Software before?

- Is everyone here in Financial Services?

- Anyone here not in Marketing?

Initial Preparation

If appropriate, and it is a small group, get people to introduce themselves. This is often beneficial to both the presenter and the other members of the audience. But keep it brief.

Often at large gatherings, name badges are provided to help identify company representatives, but these can be difficult for the presenter to see. In small groups it is easier. The presenter can read the name badges, or names can be written on cards and placed on the table in front of them. If you instruct the audience to write their names on cards, be specific. Do you want first name, surname, job title, company name?

Common ground

You may be required to give presentations to groups from different market sectors; for example, representatives from finance, sales, advertising, production.

A good presentation should be like a one-to-one conversation: the listener should feel that you are talking directly to her. The smaller the group, the easier this is to achieve. In a group with such a diversity of backgrounds, there will be different information needs.

When you are preparing your script, think of the common interests of the group. Then consider them separately, and ask again 'What's in it for them?'

One way you might deal with this situation is to give a motivational overview to the whole group. Then follow this up with separate detailed presentations. If this is not possible, you could give the information in different handouts to each group.

Group presentation

Find out if you are the only speaker. If there are other speakers:

- Know where you fit in the agenda. Are you the first speaker? If you are, will you have to deal with admin. details? Or give a general overview and introduction for the group? Will you be introduced or will you have to introduce the speaker who will follow you?
- If you are presenting the same topic, check that the information you are presenting doesn't overlap or conflict (unless by design).
- Do you have a choice of timing, i.e. morning or afternoon? If you do, ask yourself when you are at your best. Most of us have a preference. Some people are more alert first thing in the morning and for others the reverse is true. Beware the dreaded 'graveyard slot', that period after lunch when the audience is replete. You have to work extra hard here to gain audience attention.

At this stage, it is a good idea to collect your thoughts and allocate your ideas into some sort of order.

- Find out where you can get the information needed.
- Speak to people who may be able to help.
- Collect research items, books, statistics, indeed anything that may be relevant to your subject.
- Brainstorm your ideas. Jot them down as you think of them. Don't try to organise them at this stage. When you have exhausted your ideas, look at them again and see if you can link them together. Look for patterns. Do the ideas fall into general areas?
- You could draw a mind map. This will help you to see where the ideas fit.

Remember, as you work through your presentation, to have the objective in front of you. Refer to this frequently.

Initial Preparation

The next stage is to assign these ideas into roughly the following areas:
 the Opening
 the Body – key points
 the Reprise and Close.

Look at your material in relation to the objectives and the time allocated for the presentation.

Handouts

There are three major uses of handouts in a presentation:

1. to reinforce important information
2. to summarise action items for the audience to follow up
3. to supply supporting information that you don't want cluttering your visual aids.

Consider at this stage whether you will use handouts. If so, think of how many you need and also when you will give them out. This will vary, depending on the type of presentation. A general rule is that if it is not necessary for the audience to refer to the information during your talk, leave them till later. However, at large customer presentations, sales brochures and publicity materials are often available before the presentation begins. This method can elicit interest and help stimulate activity at question-time.

Always tell your audience that you have handouts for them at the beginning of your talk. If you don't, someone is sure to ask. Also, it is frustrating for the audience to jot down copious notes as you speak, only to be told at the end that the key information is covered in the handout. At very large gatherings, the audience is often given a copy of the presentation outline, and at technical presentations, the graphics used are reproduced as handouts.

Presenting For Women in Business

The following is an initial preparation checklist to help focus on some of the areas which will be developed in later chapters.

Preparation Checklist

Title of the presentation

Objective(s)

Audience – see audience profile

Time

Audience objectives (What's in it for them?)

How will I open?

What are the key points (Do I have a logical structure)?

How will I close?

How will I build rapport?

How will I add interest?

What visuals will I use?

What equipment?

How will I handle notes?

Handouts?

What are their possible questions/objections?

What approach will I take?

How will I sell the benefits?

3
Structure

All presentations may be conveniently divided into three main parts: the Opening – the Body – the Reprise and Close. These are often summarised as:

Tell them what you are going to tell them – the Opening
Tell them – the Body, including the key points
Tell them what you told them – the Reprise and Close

It's a tried and tested formula. Newsreaders use it: they open with a punchy headline, often accompanied by dramatic visuals, to gain attention. They then go into detail, developing the theme, and finish with a summing-up and close.

The time spent on each section will vary, but as a general rule and for maximum impact, spend around:

15 per cent of the total time available on the Opening
   If appropriate, inform your audience about *you*.
   Say how long you will take.
   Give ground rules for questions.
   Introduce the topic and your objectives.
   Hook their attention.

75 per cent of the time on the Body
   State your key points. As you build them up, make sure everything you say has a purpose.
   Offer evidence.
   Make it interesting.

10 per cent on the Reprise and Close
Recap the key points you made.
Make sure you put them in the context of your presentation.
Close with a strong sentence or statement.
Make your call for action.
End on a high, a positive note; never just come abruptly to an end!

There are many views on presentation length. We have all sat through presentations where the speaker has sent us to sleep after a few minutes. There are others where thirty minutes passes in a flash and the speaker leaves us wanting to hear more. Rosabeth Moss Kanter, a professor at Harvard University, is one such speaker. She always leaves the audience wanting to hear more.

Much research has gone into the subject of length. The answer that comes up most frequently as an ideal length for a presentation is seventeen minutes. Therefore your timing would be:

        Opening   —   2 minutes

        Body   —   14 minutes

        Close   —   1 minute

The first and last sentences of a presentation are crucial. The importance of a clear and resounding first sentence and a well rounded finale cannot be over-emphasised. You must capture their attention at the beginning, keep them interested throughout the body and leave them satisfied at the end.

THE OPENING

The purpose of the Opening of the presentation is to hook the attention of the audience.

The attention curve, unless specifically changed by the presenter, looks like this:

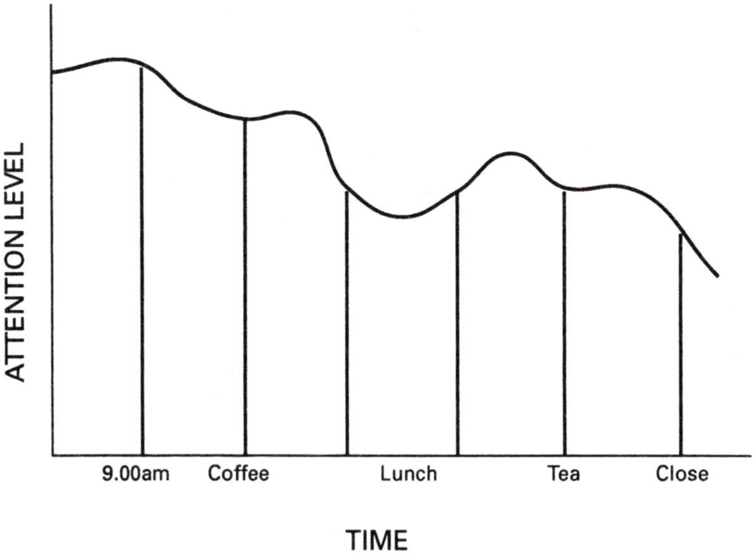
ATTENTION LEVEL
9.00am
Coffee
Lunch
Tea
Close
TIME

The attention level of the audience varies.

Interest level

Percentage of audience paying full attention

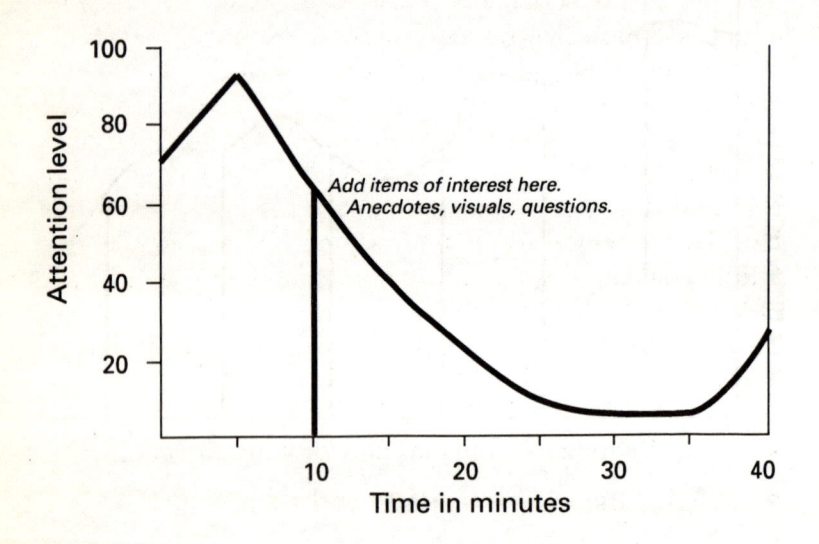

Add items of interest here. Anecdotes, visuals, questions.

(Attention level vs. Time in minutes)

Audience attention

Structure

When you step out front to begin:

- Pause and look at the audience. (This will alert them to the fact that you are about to begin.)
- Smile – providing it is not a serious topic.
- Choose the opening that is appropriate for the audience and the presentation objectives.

The hook

A hook is a statement or an object used specifically to get attention. Hooks are used, for instance, on television, radio, newspapers, magazines and billboards. Newspapers always use hooks; they're called headlines. At the time of writing, this newspaper headline has hooked my attention! MR FRISK AT RISK. It's Grand National time again, and I've drawn Mr Frisk out of the hat. This is certainly of interest, particularly when the article goes on to say that my horse may miss the chance of landing the big race double!
To help you find your hook, ask yourself the following questions:

- What is the most unusual part of your subject?
- What is the most interesting and exciting part?
- What is the most dramatic part?
- What is the most humorous part?

If any of the above are relevant to your subject, reduce each answer to a sentence. Next, look at the sentences that you have come up with, and check them against the following questions.

- Does the hook lead to your objective?
- Does the hook relate to your approach?

- Does the hook relate to your audience?
- Can the hook form the first words of your message?

The most suitable hook is one that fulfills these requirements. You will find the three-point technique useful:

Point 1 – you make an interesting impactive remark.
Point 2 – you link, skilfully, sentence one to your subject.
Point 3 – you involve the audience in both the opening remarks and your subject.

Here are some examples of types of Openings:

- **Story**
  Tell a short story that relates to your theme. Use short simple sentences and get to the point quickly. A personal experience told as a story can create intimacy with your listeners. Sometimes I say, 'A friend of mine and I once had a discussion on whether it was possible to combine a career and a family successfully. Perhaps some of you have considered this when...' Revealing something personal creates closeness with the audience. Audiences love self-disclosure as long as it is relevant to the subject.

- **Quotation**
  Keep quotations short and use them only if they are relevant to your subject. Try and attribute the quotation to its true author. If in doubt, you could try: 'Was it Oscar Wilde who said...' or, 'I believe it was Winston Churchill who once remarked that...' If you are attributing the quote to someone in your own lifetime, try 'I once heard Mel Gibson remark that...' This goes down well, and nobody can disprove it!

- **Question**
  'Do you know what most women fear the most? According to studies, it is the fear of speaking before an audience.'

Structure

- **Direct statement of thesis**
  'It is my belief that more women would return to work if better childcare facilities were available.'

- **Startling statement**
  'Did you know that employee theft in the UK is running at £830 million per year?'

- **Statement to be opposed**
  'David Brown has said that employee morale has not declined over the last year . . . I am here today to prove to you this is not so.'

- **Unusual fact**
  'A Gallup survey found that fat bosses rate slimline power-dressing above talent (maybe not so unusual).'

- **Statement of assumption**
  'Contrary to popular opinion, women make excellent presenters.'

- **Explanation of a title**
  '*Good Business* . . . is an interesting book which examines . . .'

- **Definition of terms**
  'Perseverance is the phenomenon of continuing . . . even though you cannot . . .'

- **Statement of need or problem**
  'The situation is this . . .'

- **Use an exhibit/model/visual**
  'The printer you see here . . .'

- **Show how subject can affect the audience**
  'Computer software theft is currently . . . We need to reduce this figure by . . . Failure to do so will adversely affect . . .'

The Opening of a presentation should be well prepared in advance. A positive opening will hook the audience attention for what will follow. Here are some pointers:

Greet the audience warmly
Look and sound happy to be talking to them. Face them and give good eye contact.

Hook
Start with your hook. Speak to the back of the room. Be clear and positive.

Introduction
Tell them your name and, if relevant, your job title, company, and a little background information about yourself. (This helps establish credibility.) Usually the presenter has been asked to give the presentation because she is the person who has expertise in the subject to be presented. This should be brief, and should raise the comfort level of the audience, i.e. here is someone who sounds knowledgeable.

Subject
Give them the title of your presentation and make it provocative. The title acts as a stimulus; it should play to your purpose and, ideally, your point.

Give your audience clear signposts. Tell them where you intend to take them within your subject. Signposting establishes several important factors. It shows that you know where you are going, and that there is a logical progression within your talk; and it also defines the limits in which you will work.

Tell them how long the presentation will last.

Other
Set the ground rules for questions. Decide if you will take them during the presentation or afterwards and inform the audience. You will be more in control of timing if you

Structure

take questions at the end. However, it is often beneficial to invite questions throughout the presentation, particularly if the subject matter involves detailed or technical information.

Tell the audience if you have materials to give them. Only give them out at this point if they need to refer to them during the presentation.

THE BODY

'All speech, written or spoken, is a dead language, until it finds a willing and prepared hearer.'
Robert Louis Stevenson

You have now introduced yourself and your subject to the audience. Their attention has been hooked and they are interested to hear what you have to say.

Now follows the Body, or meat, of the presentation. This section should continue to hold audience interest as well as put across information, arguments, and key points related to the subject. The 'Body' should follow a logical sequence with frequent signposts, leading the audience towards the objectives. Research shows that the attention span of an audience varies at different times of the day: for example, high attention levels at the beginning of the day, after coffee; and low before breaks, after lunch and late afternoon. Often the post-lunch session is favoured for a demonstration, a discussion session, or a question and answer period; anything, in fact, to involve the audience in activity.

You may not have a choice of presentation time. The presenter, therefore, has to work to keep the attention level high. There are many ways to add interest to the Body; choose which is the most appropriate for the occasion. The following are some suggestions.

Humour

Don't use humour just for the sake of it. If it is appropriate for your topic and audience, then use it carefully. There are several points to watch here:

- Make sure that your jokes are in good taste (not sexist, racist, ageist). If there is any doubt that they might give offence, even to only a few members of the audience, leave them out.
- An original joke is best, because your audience will not have heard it before. Keep clear of puns and clichés.
- The safest joke is a joke against yourself.

Finally, your jokes must have some bearing on the subject you are talking about. Humorous stories are a valuable addition to most presentations, as long as they observe the above rules.

Examples

Examples are an excellent way of keeping attention and interest. A good example should follow these two guidelines:

- The example should be a typical, not exceptional, one.
- Use enough examples to constitute a fair sample. You may need to use additional statistical information to support the conclusions you draw from one example.

Statistics

- Make them meaningful. For example, 'Fraud in the City of London is estimated to cost £500 million a

Structure

year. That means that every employee is losing £10 a week in wages as a result of crime.'

- Use only a few statistics at a time. Break the monotony of listing statistics by using an anecdote or a visual aid.
- Use visuals to present statistics. Write large bold figures on the flipchart. To dramatise figures, use pictures and symbols instead of words.

Support material

This can make the simplest, most ordinary talk interesting. Presenters who produce interesting support material to clarify and prove their main ideas sound more authentic and lively.

Bear in mind that your presentation will be as interesting as its supporting material. Now is the time to get down to facts, cases, illustrations. Use them to clarify and, with the use of reasoning, prove your points. Visual aids will help you connect and link ideas together and we will look at these in a later chapter.

Tricks of the trade

Another way of holding audience attention is to vary the way that you present the information. For example, when presenting information, use the format: **Major idea** – Detail – Detail – **Recap**.

For bad news, or to persuade: **Hint** – Detail – Detail – Detail – **Major idea** – **Recap**.

To present ideas to management, there is a simple mnemonic: Preface, Position, Problem, Possibility, Proposal, Postscript.

If what you propose has a limitation, present it in the first half of your sentence, and then present the benefits which will trade that off. *Always* put the limitation first.

THE REPRISE AND CLOSE

Many presenters start working on the Close of the presentation before any other area, and work backwards; the ending should be brief and bold.

Types of Close
Ask the audience to take some specific action.
Outline alternative actions for the audience.
Express confidence in what the audience will do about the matter.
Express confidence that the problem will be resolved.

Other endings
Use a suitable quotation from someone known to the audience, or from literature.
Use an illustration.
End with a humorous story.

Your closing remarks are your last chance to convey the message; so recap your main points (Reprise).

Avoid such anticlimactic closes as 'Thank you very much.' You may wish to compliment the audience, but make sure that you are sincere.

End on a high or positive note. Once you have raised your audience to a high pitch, stop – sit down.

Now that you have a clear presentation structure, it is time to draft your script.

Checklist of the five key elements to audience interest and recall

Power
Begin powerfully. Everything about you should come across as being positive, including your stance, your voice. Let your enthusiasm show. Let your audience see how happy you are

Structure

to be talking to them. Communicate with your audience – don't lecture them. Involve them as soon as possible.

Repeat
Your audience will be better able to remember points that you repeat regularly. Commercial advertisers use this technique. Count the number of times the product name or telephone number is repeated in a short space of time. It could be a phrase or a saying.

Emphasise
Stimulate your audience; present your facts in a variety of ways which will help them remember your key points.

Maximise involvement
Ask rhetorical questions to increase audience interest and attention.

Go out with a bang
Make the ending unforgettable!

4
Putting Your Notes Together

>'Think like a listener.
>Write like a good talker.'
>*Anon.*

The following are some hints on putting your script together and finally developing that script into notes. Written speeches may be appropriate for the Prime Minister and Government Ministers when addressing the nation, but when used on any other occasion, such as presentations to potential clients or company annual meetings, they can be dull.

Drafting and Scripting

In the brainstorming session, you will have identified several areas to be covered and your key points. If it is a subject which you are talking about for the first time, write out the speech in full. You will find that, even for a short presentation, you will fill several sheets of paper with ideas.

Editing

Presenters often have difficulty in editing their script down to manageable size. The following simple guidelines will help you to do this. Take into account: the time you have available to present; your objectives; and the audience objectives. Then, look through the brainstorm notes you made during the initial preparation. Look at your ideas one at a time and ask yourself, 'If I include this information, will it take me towards the objectives?'. In

Presenting For Women in Business

```
                    Audience
                    objectives

                   Information

         Nice to know
          * Should know
             **Must** know
             (essential
             information)

* Information could be given as handout
```

Editing

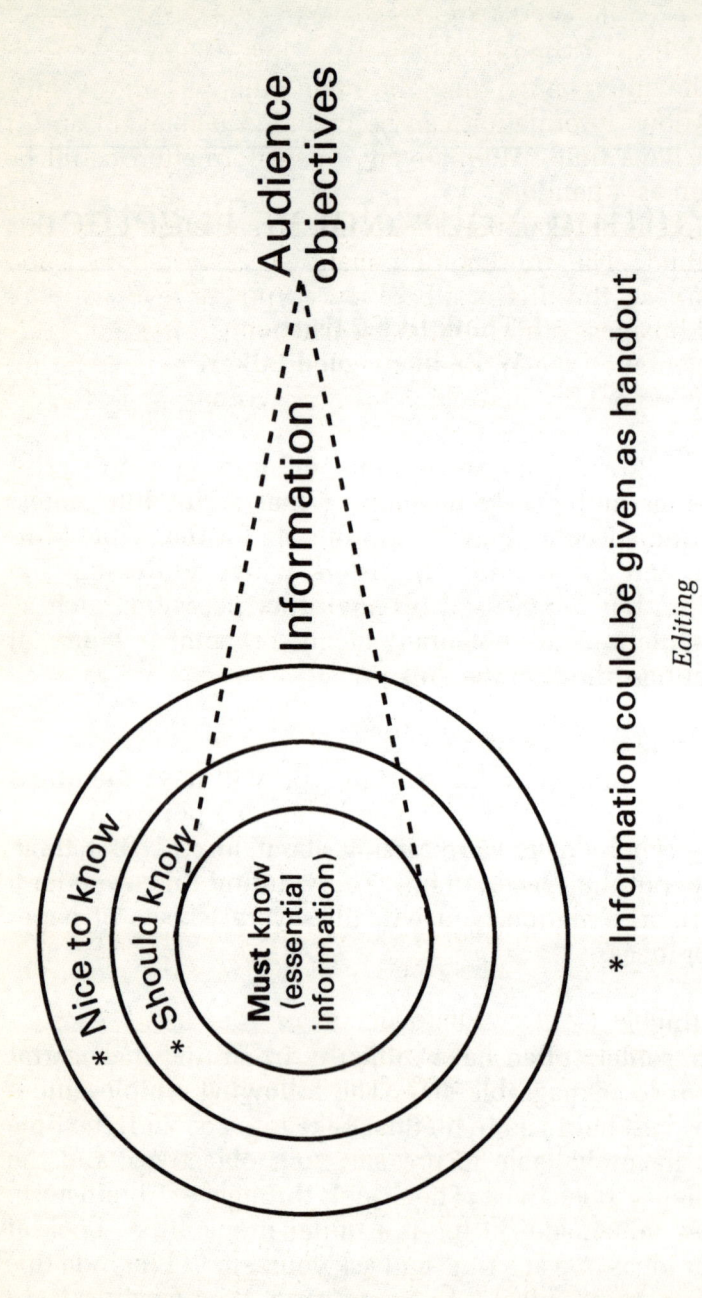

Putting Your Notes Together

other words, do the audience need to know this information? If so, it should be included. This is often referred to as the 'must know' rule. The 'should know' and the 'nice to know' information can be included if relevant and if you have time. Alternatively, this information could be given as a handout.

Here is an example of editing a presentation using this method. The presentation material is based on *Good Business*, the title of a book on corporate responsibility and business ethics. In the brainstorming session for this presentation, there was enough material and ideas for several books – impossible to cover in the time available! It is important that this vast topic, intended as a general overview of business ethics, be broken up into subheadings, bearing in mind the objectives and also the presentation time of 45 minutes.

Sample Presentation

Title: The Ethical Edge

Objectives: To inform the audience of the benefits of adopting an ethical approach to business

Time: 45 minutes

Audience: All company managing directors, chief executives and management personnel

Subject matter:
1. *Introduction to business ethics*
   - The lean organisation
   - Culture
   - Fairness

2. *Ethics are the key*
   - Ethics as ground rules
   - Best results ethics

3. *Developing a code of ethics*
   - Method
   - Implementation

As you can see, the topic has been divided up into three key areas: introduction to business ethics; ethics are the key; and developing a code of ethics. The key points in each area will be covered under their respective headings and these *headings* and *key points* will now form the basis for your notes.

NOTES VERSUS CARDS

Remember that you have decided on this structure:

Opening – Body (key points) – Reprise and Close

- Concentrate on your Close first. At the end of the presentation, what is the message you want ringing in the ears of your audience? Jot this down, then work through the rest of your script.
- The development or Body section will consist of your key points. This is the information that you have decided *must* be included. Brief headings are sufficient here. Think of the links between each point. This will direct the flow of speech, but not interrupt it.

Whether you use notes or cards is a matter of choice. If well managed, both can be effective. The following observations may help you to decide which will suit you best.

Putting Your Notes Together

Using cards

'Organisation is the key to clarity.'

Postcard-sized cards are a useful aid:

- Use one side only.
- Write each theme/idea on a separate card.
- When you have covered the information on the card, turn over.
- Number each card and leave loose. Alternatively, use a binder clip in one corner. You can then slip your thumb through this. (Cards can thus be kept in order.)
- Especially easy to handle are 4 × 6 inch cards on which the outline is typed vertically. These can be held in your hand like a pack of playing cards.

The benefits of using cards far outweigh the disadvantages of the time it takes to prepare them. They are neat and can be handled discreetly; they are also flexible. For instance, if you find yourself running out of time you can skip one or two cards (or summarise each card in a sentence). Moreover, you can hold them if you need to walk around.

Sheets of paper

These are more visible. Avoid scraps, or large wodges, of paper and do not hold a single piece of paper in your hand (if you are nervous, shaking paper is more evident).

- If there are only a few sheets of paper, place a firm card at the back (if you are going to hold them).
- If using a table lectern, number each sheet in the top left-hand corner. Display two sheets at once. Practise

the smooth sliding over of the next sheet. This reduces the rustling effect which often accompanies the handling of notes.
- Leave sufficient space between ideas so that you can read the information easily.

Whether you are using cards or notes, make them work for you. Never use material that other people have written, unless it is adapted to your style of delivery and is appropriate to the audience and subject.

Avoid slang, jargon, swear words, and also technical language if speaking to a non-technical audience.

General hints

- Draw a margin down one side of the page or card and use this to illustrate where, for example, you will show an overhead slide, write on flip, give a handout.
- Use a red pen to underline key words. Make additional red check marks next to ideas that need emphasis.
- Underline the opening phrase in each paragraph with a highlighter pen.
- Having visual aids is another means of using notes: slides and charts can serve as an outline and information source for you.
- You can pencil notes in flipchart margins or overhead frames without your audience knowing it.

Your notes are an aid, not a hindrance. Make them brief, uncluttered and use language that is simple to understand. You have now:

evaluated your material
eliminated unnecessary information

Putting Your Notes Together

Avoid logorrhea!

grouped your ideas together
structured the information, with a punchy introduction
developed a logical sequence
decided on your Close
assembled your notes.

DEVELOP YOUR SCRIPT

The next stage is actually to read the presentation out loud from your notes. You will quickly realise that the written word is not always suitable for speech. A good presentation should be delivered in conversational style; so in the final script add the light and shade to the written word for delivery.

When reading your presentation out loud you will have noticed points, words and phrases that need emphasis and points where you need to pause. You may also find words/phrases which looked good in written form, but don't sound right. Use this information to develop your script, for example, underline words that you need to emphasise with a red pen and mark the pauses on your script. Punctuation is critical. Use short sentences; however, it will sound boring if all the sentences are short, so vary their length without sacrificing the meaning.

When you have completed your script, staple the sheets together or use the card ring. Then rehearse, rehearse... I recently attended a large presentation where the presenters included many prominent names in the business world. After one particular presenter had finished his presentation and just before the coffee break, the audience (150 people) were given copies of his presentation. Unfortunately, we had copies of his own actual script:
'Good morning ladies and gentlemen (PAUSE) I am *delighted* to...'!

Putting Your Notes Together

Do you need a full script? These guidelines, based on experience, may help you decide.

A **full script** is advisable when:

- the occasion is formal
- the presentation will be recorded
- the material is complex
- the sequence of audio-visual aids requires fixed cues for the projectionist.
- the presenter is inexperienced.

Brief notes are recommended when:

- the occasion is not too formal
- the presentation will not be recorded
- the material does not demand a full script
- the speaker is relatively experienced.

Short headings are adequate when:

- the occasion is informal
- the presentation will not be recorded
- the material is relatively simple
- the speaker is very experienced.

Text layout

The following are some recommendations:

Use large type

A word processor can help you to achieve the type style you require. Major typewriter manufacturers also have a variety of type size and style options. Normal print style using upper and lower case 'letter' size can be enlarged, using the 'blow-up' technique. Many printers offer this service.

Limit the number of words per line
Try not to have more than eight or nine words on a line. This will enable you comfortably to 'photograph' mentally roughly a line at a time.

Avoid breaking words
Keep words intact. It is far better to carry the whole word to the next line, leaving extra space, than to break the word with a hyphen. Even compound words with hyphens should be kept intact on one line.

Use wide margins
Side margins should be at least one inch on each side. Top and bottom margins should be closer to an inch and a half. This will give you a lot of 'white space' around your script, making the print stand out more.

Line spacing
You should at least double-space each line. This will vary with type style. For example, if you are using all capital letters, triple-spacing would be better.

Sentence spacing
Make sure that between each full point and the start of a new sentence you have a good separation so that there is a clear break. Normally, this will be two or three spaces. Again, this will vary with type style.

Paragraph spacing
This will also vary with type style. As a general rule, spacing between paragraphs should be wider than your line spacing.

Putting Your Notes Together

Indent each paragraph
This will increase the amount of 'white space' on the page, making it easier for you to keep your place and take your time.

End each page with a full point
Never carry a sentence from the bottom of one page to the top of the next. Doing so causes needless delivery problems.

Start each page with a new paragraph
As no sentences are carried over from page to page, every page starts with a new sentence, which should be indented as a new paragraph. This will give you a sense of timing for a smooth page transition, as well as additional 'white space'.

Avoid long sentences and paragraphs
Long sentences should be shortened to two, or even three, shorter sentences. Long paragraphs should be split into shorter, more easily handled paragraphs. This will reduce the chances of losing your place.

One-sentence paragraphs
Making a key sentence a separate paragraph helps you give it the emphasis it deserves.

Marking your script
Suspension points (...) can be used in many places instead of commas. This will improve the layout physically by providing more 'white space' which will give you a better sense of time. Underlining key words or phrases can also help you visually. Avoid using slashes (/) to indicate pauses, which may produce a mechanical or unnatural delivery.

Visual aid cues

You should clearly indicate on your script when a visual aid should be displayed and when it should be removed. This is best done in capital letters, underlined, and should be placed in the middle of the page . . . not to the side. For example,

SLIDE ON

As far as spacing is concerned, the cue instruction should be treated as a paragraph:

SLIDE OFF

Page numbers

Page numbers can either be centred at the top of the page or placed in the two top corners.

Bifocal lenses

For those who have bifocal lenses, it might be easier to limit the printed information to the upper half or two-thirds of the page.

TIMING

> **'The point of satiation is reached very soon after the peak of popularity.'**
>
> Dr Johnson

Time limitation

Do you have ten minutes or twenty minutes or forty minutes? Always know how long you should speak.

When you first start to rehearse your presentation you will find that timing is difficult to gauge accurately. You have edited your material so you know that the information you put across will be relevant (no waffle). When you put your notes together, mark time checks on each page or card. One key point per card will help you do this.

Putting Your Notes Together

Allocate the elapsed time from the start to the climax of each key point. Do not use actual times, as start time for presentations can run early or late. Mark these times on your notes, say every three minutes for a short presentation or five for a longer one. As you progress through the presentation you can slow down, speed up, cut; introduce extra items as necessary in order to finish at the exact time. Rehearse your presentation until your timing is right.

The following may help you to get your timing under control:

- A rate of speech test
- A readability test

Rate of speech test

The average rate of speech is approximately 150 words per minute. Speaking rapidly makes it difficult for others to understand you, and speaking very slowly may cause others to lose patience and stop listening attentively.

To check your rate of speech, read the following article aloud and time yourself. The article contains about 300 words, and it should take two minutes to read at the rate of 150 words a minute. You may wish to use a tape recorder.

Speech, at the most elementary level, demands extensive mental effort. A meaning, before it takes form in speech, is something which is not yet defined. Its communication in speech requires that it be conveyed in some kind of order.

The simple fact is that we rarely achieve a continuous flow of speech. The speaker and the listener cooperate. Listeners concentrate on the message: they integrate elements of the message; they bridge the gaps which divide the groups of words. The speaker, on the other hand, cooperates by trying to minimise the gaps in the stream of words and to make them coincide with semantic groups such as phrases.

The point to remember is that pausing is as much a part of speaking as vocal utterance. Pausing is a very basic part of speech production and has a specific function in the giving of a presentation. It permits delay – the time for thinking, for the thought process to take place. There is no need to substitute 'ah', 'er', and 'um', 'well', 'now', and the like. The listener will not find the pause unusual. Delay is simply a built-in feature of oral language. Most pauses go unnoticed because they are natural, so there is no reason to have a continuous flow of sound while speaking.

Concentrate on the idea you are dealing with, gain confidence and a sense of rapport with your audience, and your hesitations will be no longer than the minimal delays which we have come to expect, and in fact need, in spontaneous speech. Pace should not be dictated by the pressure of time on the day itself. This means constant practice before your presentation. Speak out loud in your normal voice. You can then change your script where appropriate.

End of test

Now check your rate. If your rate of speech is very much lower than 120–150 words per minute, practise until you are happy with it. Also check that your script is working for you. Do you have pauses, emphasis marked? Listen to your tape recording. Would that voice make you sit up and take notice?

Readability test

Often copies of the presentation script are given to the audience after the event. Will your audience recognise it

Putting Your Notes Together

as the performance you gave? A readability test is useful to check the written materials which are distributed.

The purpose of this test is to measure how easy or difficult it is to read a piece of your writing. As a measure of readability, it is based on two factors: sentence length and word length.

What to do

1. Take a sample of your own writing, such as a letter, memo or report. The sample should be at least 200 words long.

2. Count the number of words in the passage and divide this by the number of sentences to give the average words per sentence. Count hyphenated words as two, and treat as words such items as numbers and symbols.

3. Count the number of long words, i.e. words of three or more syllables. Disregard capitalised proper names and also words of which the third syllable is one of the grammatical suffixes: '-ed' (invited), '-es' (supposes) or '-ing' (presenting). Work out the total number of long words as a percentage of all the words in the piece.

4. Add together the two figures, i.e. average words per sentence and the percentage of long words, and this gives you your readability index. It is probably between 25 and 40. The lower the figure, the more easily understandable the piece is likely to be.

5. Repeat this exercise with further samples of your own writing, and take a final score.

Sentence length and word length are not the only factors affecting readability, so the index figure may be misleading. Also important are:

- right choice of words
- sentence structure
- style of language (appropriate to reader)
- clear layout, use of headings and paragraphs
- interesting subject
- punctuation

Your average sentence length should be about 20 and never rise above 30 words. But if you try and write all sentences to have a length of about 20 words, the result will be a very stilted style. Just write naturally with no rules in mind, and if the result is rather turgid to read, then take a look at the length of sentences to see if some need pruning.

Perhaps it is taking a liberty to classify all three-syllable words as long; for example, 'area' has three syllables but only four letters! But the criterion works usefully for the purpose of this exercise. It is not that three-syllable or long words are difficult or unusual. It probably struck you that some of those you counted were straightforward, everyday terms that will puzzle nobody. The point is, a piece of writing becomes heavy to read if it contains a concentration of long words, however simple these words may be individually.

Your percentage of long words should normally be about 10 per cent or less. If it is approaching 15 per cent and there is no way of avoiding it (say, because of the technical nature of the subject) then consider using shorter sentences to help compensate. Your readability index is a useful guide, but the only true test of a piece's readability is how it actually reads.

Compare your score with the following:

The Sun	26%
Daily Mirror	28%

Putting Your Notes Together

Sunday Times Business News	30%
Daily Mail	31%
Daily Telegraph	34%
The Guardian	39%
Conditions of use on application for Access card	49%

5
Communication

> 'Courage comes from wanting to say it well; security comes from knowing you can say it well; confidence comes from having said it well.'
>
> *Anon.*

On the face of it, after all your preparation is done, communicating the message should be easy. There are, however, many things which can inhibit good communications with your audience.

When you speak to an audience, many factors are combining to convey a message about you (the speaker). These include your posture, your gestures, your clothes, your accent, your reputation, and several others. These should not work in opposition to your message.

Barriers to receiving the message that you are putting across include the listeners' needs, their anxieties and expectations. If they do not get what they want in this respect, then it will be difficult for you to communicate with them. Different cultural backgrounds and traditions can give people a different value system; different political views can change attitudes to the speaker. All of these can inhibit the communication process.

So, the first step to good communication is to **know your audience**, be aware of the above and try to understand their needs. That way you can establish the wavelength on which you will speak.

Presenting For Women in Business

Hostility signified by:
- Aggressive posture
- Harsh tone of voice
- 'Set' mouth
- Distance
- Staring eyes

Submissiveness signified by:
- Speaking quietly/ saying little
- Allowing interruptions
- Meek tone of voice
- Poor eye contact
- 'Handwashing' and other nervous gestures

Warmth signified by:
- Sympathetic gestures
- Proximity
- Relaxed tone of voice
- Good eye contact
- Expansive gestures

Control/domination signified by:
- Speaking loudly/ quickly all the time
- Ignoring responses
- Interrupting
- 'Controlling' tone of voice
- 'Stabbing' fingers and other forceful gestures

Non-verbal communications

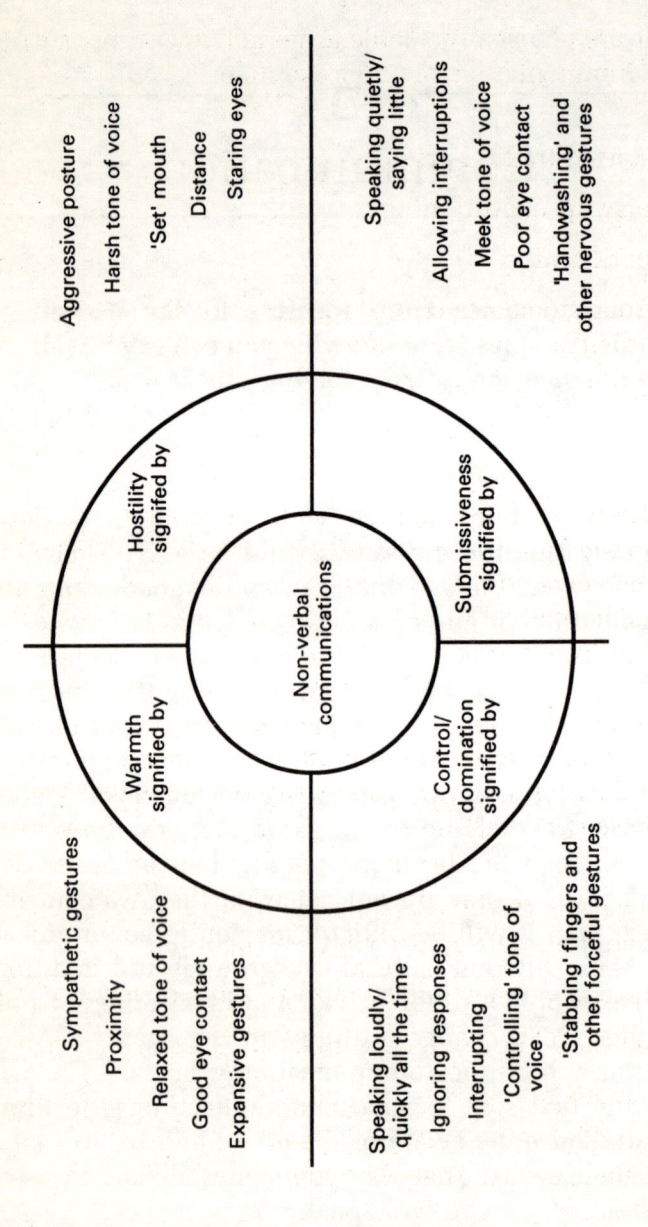

Assess the image you project. Could it be improved?

Communication

BARRIERS TO EFFECTIVE COMMUNICATION

People are physically unable to see and hear properly due to environmental factors. For example:

- external traffic noise
- noisy air conditioning
- poor lighting
- wrong room layout or equipment for the size of audience
- room temperature too hot or cold, as a result of which the audience switches off.

Sometimes the audience are unable to concentrate when they cannot see the relevance of the subject; they may perceive that it has no interest or significance to them. Alternatively, the language used may not be understood or the presenter may be giving mixed messages.

Emotions, prejudices, assumptions can cloud the intended message, because people will attend the presentation with their own views on the subject being presented. The following will help you clarify the steps that you, as the presenter, must take:

- Always begin by correctly identifying with the needs of your audience, i.e. what are *their* objectives?
- Make fewer statements and ask *more* questions.
- Sell them the benefits which will satisfy their needs.
- Demonstrate how these benefits will be delivered.
- Relate to them as individuals and appeal to their values and aspirations. If what you say goes against their beliefs, it will be resisted.

The actual language you use can also be a barrier to good communications. This is particularly true when the language of the presentation is a foreign one (i.e. not the mother tongue of the audience). Do not speak very slowly or shout at them to compensate; they are not stupid or deaf, but they may need a little more time to digest the information. Give them ample opportunity to ask questions for clarification. This is equally true when you are presenting technical material, or introducing new ideas.

Some years ago I travelled to the Netherlands to train a group of salespeople in presentation skills. Shortly after the introduction to the programme, I noticed that, although they appeared interested, a few of the participants were leafing through books open on their tables. Later, I discovered that they were looking up the precise meanings of words in their dictionaries. Apparently, one of their objectives in attending the course was to brush up on their English!

So perhaps we should also remember to look for the hidden agenda. Use positive and motivating words. If the message you have to put across is potentially negative, try and turn it into a positive. The attitude of your audience is a reflection of your own attitude. A positive approach produces positive results.

Listen to facts and feelings and respond in kind. Cultivate a positive attitude. Angela Rumbold, MP recently addressed a Conference with the words, 'Your attitude determines your altitude.' There is a lot of truth in this. A positive mental attitude is contagious; it can rub off on your audience.

Eliminate environmental barriers to reception of the message. For example, if there are more interesting things going on outside the room, if the room is excessively hot, cold or badly ventilated, the communication process will be impaired.

The right attitude on the part of the presenter can:

Communication

- build communication bridges with the audience
- develop audience rapport
- foster a good communications environment

Having PMA (a positive mental attitude) will also help.

> **'Begin low, speak slow, take fire, rise higher.**
> **When must impress be self possessed,**
> **At the end wax warm, and sit down in a storm.'**
> *Anon.*

Speaking is about the strength of your enthusiasm. It is only effective when you let your enthusiasm and commitment drive your ideas and actions. Speaking starts deep inside the mind and the body. Effective communication is achieved when the whole body talks with authority and confidence.

VOICE AND DELIVERY

The person who speaks softly is judged to be shy;
the person who speaks loudly is judged to be aggressive or bold;
the person who speaks in a moderate tone is judged to be neither too shy nor too bold.

Observing good presenters, you will almost certainly see that they are committed to their words. They show enthusiasm for what they say and how they say it. Speaking in a monotone is tedious for the audience and is sure to send them to sleep.

In speaking, you can:

- vary the speed of delivery
- introduce effective pauses

- alter volume and pitch
- emphasise particular words or phrases
- employ gestures or convey meaning by expression.

A good presenter will employ all the above techniques in the presentation, thereby adding light and shade to the words and making them 'live' for the audience.

Volume
Do you pronounce words distinctly or speak too softly? This can be due to talking with tight lips. Open your mouth wider. Many speech experts believe that failure to project is linked with improper breathing and/or poor posture. Take a deep breath before you speak and between sentences.

Pitch
Do you speak in a monotone? Does your voice drop at the end of sentences? Use more questions instead of statements, because questions tend to end at a higher pitch.

Enunciation
This is the formation of particular speech sounds. Use your dictionary as your guide for all pronunciations. And, for terms that have different 'correct' pronunciations you should aim for consistency.

Speed
The human mind processes words at approximately 500 a minute, and we speak at about 150 words a minute – a difference of 350. If any of the communication barriers are at work, the audience will shut off and become preoccupied with their own thoughts. This is often referred to as travelling down route 350!

Decide how you might vary your rate of speaking at different points in your presentation. You may want to

Communication

pause slightly before or after important words and slow down for complicated phrases or words that have particular meaning. John F. Kennedy used this ploy: he would speak several words with great rapidity, come to the word or phrase he wished to emphasise, and let his voice linger and bear hard on that. Then he would rush to the end of his sentence like lightning. He would devote as much time to the word or two he wished to emphasise as he did to half a dozen less important words surrounding it. Such a method invariably arrests attention. Try saying the following: 'fifty million pounds'. Say it quickly and with a throwaway, inconsequential air so that it sounds a small sum. Now say: 'fifty thousand pounds'. Say it slowly; say it with feeling; say it as if you were tremendously impressed with the hugeness of the amount. Haven't you now made the fifty thousand pounds sound larger than the fifty million?

PROJECTION

> **'My dear mother-in-law only projects her voice when calling for a gin!'**
>
> *Michael Aspel*

However much you change the volume and tone of your presentation, you must be heard. If possible, do your rehearsal in the room where you will speak. Rehearse your presentation and speak to the back of the room – imagine it extends beyond that boundary. Project clearly, but try not to shout. If possible, get someone to sit at the back of the room while you rehearse; that way you can get some feedback. Be careful not to drop your voice at the end of sentences. In fact, the last few words spoken should be loud and clear.

Richard Burton achieved his gritty tones by going up into the mountains and shouting at sheep. National and regional accents can also produce interest. Gone are the days of the standard BBC accent. This is apparent in the media and also among actors (unless they intend to join the RSC!) We all have accents: they are part of us, of our personality. However, having an accent is only a plus if our speech can be understood by the listener.

Many presenters report their voices sounding squeaky. Women are often accused of sounding shrill, which may be due to inadequate breath control. You need air to make a sound. To make loud sounds you therefore need plenty of air and you need to ration it as you speak. If you run out of breath, your voice comes out jerky and weak.

If you have trouble catching your breath as you speak, try this calm-breathing exercise:

> Stand up straight and put your hand flat against your diaphragm (that large muscle below your rib cage). Without raising your shoulders, take a deep inward breath. If your chest expands, your diaphragm will move down and your hand will move out when you breathe in. That means that you are breathing correctly. If the hand on your diaphragm is not moving out as you inhaled, you may be having breathing problems. Again, inhale as you push your hand out. Practise this exercise several times daily so that you can move your muscles to make room for more air in your lungs.

Remember that responsibility for clear communication lies with the communicator. Follow the advice given here to improve this communication process. But remember, the receiver or 'audience' has to:

- hear or see what is said or shown
- understand what is meant
- accept or agree with what was meant
- take the right action subsequently.

Communication

Projection checklist

- Use the outward breath, relax and begin.
- Give them good eye contact.
- Start positively and loudly.
- Speak clearly, control your speed.
- Pause, when appropriate, for understanding and before and after your important ideas.
- Stress the important words and give less attention to the unimportant ones.
- Let the pitch of your voice flow up and down the scale from high to low and back again, just as the pitch of a little child does when speaking.

BUILDING CREDIBILITY

Many presenters feel anxious about being credible and able to influence. Your audience needs to trust you before you can influence them. Ultimately your own motives, willingness to help and actual behaviour will determine the level of trust. In order to influence your audience, you must make a favourable impact at the first meeting so that they are willing to continue to listen. Rapport is about building communication bridges with your audience. Through your verbal and non-verbal communication, you are connecting with every member of your audience. At the same time, your audience should feel that you are genuinely interested in them and their concerns.

Build trust at an early stage of the presentation by forming a rapport with the audience and having a good sense of timing, knowing when to take charge and when to let others have their turn. If you try to dominate all the time, you may lose your effectiveness.

Presenting For Women in Business

To form rapport:

- Smile and look pleasant.
- Check your body language.
- Reveal something personal about yourself (something they can relate to).
- Relate to them and/or their company.
- If it's a small group and you know names, use them.
- Give them good eye contact.
- Involve the audience, e.g. ask questions.

Quite often, your feelings about tackling a subject stem from memories of past experiences. If these experiences were not positive, then anxiety can set in. Sometimes it is necessary to pre-programme our feelings; for example, if we are involved in a car accident, we don't want to get back behind the wheel. (Often we are persuaded otherwise.) What we are doing is replaying the feelings we felt at that time. It's similar to replaying a tape, only the second time *you* can dictate the outcome.

Many sports coaches train their athletes in this way. Billie-Jean King, former ladies' tennis champion, is no exception. She said that before every important game she would spend the evening sitting in an armchair and visualising the match. She imagined each serve or return of her opponent and then imagined her own reaction to her opponent's ball. It meant that when Billie-Jean got on court her mind was pre-programmed to cope with any situation. Regardless of what her opponent did with the ball, she would know how to handle it. In fact, she automatically played her best shot to handle the situation, because she was programmed to do so. Later, she would watch the replay on video to see where she could play better; you could say she was mentally replaying those situations which called for better strategy or

Communication

control of the ball. Thus she was again programming her mind to deal automatically with such situations when they occurred in a future game. Maxwell Maltz also uses this method and advises salespeople on the importance of creating a positive mental attitude. In preparation for giving a presentation, developing a self-fulfilling prophecy means *knowing and believing* that your presentation will be good. After all, you have seen the tapes!

> **'A woman is like a teabag. Only in hot water, do you realise how strong she is.'**
> *Nancy Reagan*

Keep up that PMA even when things go wrong. Don't draw attention to the fact. I can recall one presenter who stopped halfway through his talk and gasped, 'I've lost a slide'. Much fumbling followed, and eventually he gave up searching and continued. The feedback from the group later was, 'If you hadn't drawn attention to the problem, we wouldn't have noticed!' This is true with many of the little things which can go amiss. Thorough preparation will take care of most eventualities, but if not, then this is the time to use humour against yourself. Remember that providing you have established rapport with the group they will be rooting for you and willing you to succeed. It's the way that you handle the situation that's important.

A famous actor did just this. He addressed his audience of 200 people with enthusiasm. He then dropped his script. His poetry reading depended on this vital information! With a flourish he picked it up from the stage and shouted to the back of the hall, 'I'll start again!' He then proceeded, to the sound of applause from the audience.

Movement should be purposeful. Anyone who has done any acting will be familiar with the word 'blocking', i.e. obscuring someone or something else. So during rehearsals the actors practise what positions they should be in at each stage of the performance. It is the same with presentations. You, as the presenter, should build in at least some of the movement which will occur; for example, at which side of the screen you will stand to show the overheads. Plan the relationships between your items of equipment in order to add variety to your movement. If your movement is not purposeful, it will become a distraction.

The presenter who delivers her presentation in an enthusiastic manner will find that she will scarcely need to concentrate on varying the tone of her voice. This will happen automatically. The same applies to movement and gesture. Any movement which is repeated without purpose will become mannerism; for example, pacing up and down in front of the audience, playing with pens, notes or other objects, wringing hands, crossing legs, clearing throat and many more.

Eliminate the negative. Here are a couple of phrases heard from presenters: 'This is a pretty boring topic.' (An accountant explaining department expenditure.) 'You probably can't read this slide at the back of the room.' (Senior manager briefing staff.)

Your behaviour, together with your appearance, is the only part of you that other people can see. No one can ever see your motives, your thoughts, your attitudes or your feelings; people can only see the behaviour that results from these things. Your behaviour is directly observable by other people. The conclusions other people reach about you are based on your behaviour. The conclusions may not be accurate, of course, but the fact remains that their judgements have to be based on what they observe.

6
Body Language

The loudest statement a speaker makes is emitted before she opens her mouth: she tells the audience with a whole series of signals how she feels. If the message conveyed is nervous, vulnerable and weak, then everything that follows is transmitted in that frequency, and consequently fails to make an impact.

When

Consciously use it:

- to set the scene so as to relax the recipient (e.g. at a selection interview) or to alert them to your feelings (e.g. when about to give praise, criticism)
- to give feedback (e.g. I am listening, interested, concerned, enthusiastic – or not!)
- to invite a response or a contribution
- to develop empathy and build trusting relationships
- to present yourself effectively – develop your image and self-confidence, beat the stereotype. Remember, first impressions last.

How much

Don't overdo it: stay within the limits where you and the recipient feel comfortable and remember that uncalled for displays of body language create unnecessary risk.

How

Keep your chin up, literally. Let your non-verbals be seen and heard – don't reduce your body language, even on the telephone. Research conducted by Albert Mehrabian shows that the sum of the message you communicate is made up as follows:

- 55% Appearance and Body Language
- 38% How you sound
- 7% What you say

It follows, therefore, that if we look good, use positive body language, sound enthusiastic about our subject, and are well prepared, we will present a very powerful message! However, this only holds true when we are talking about first impressions – those vital seconds when you are standing before an audience for the first time. You may look the part and sound enthusiastic about your subject, but if poor preparation and delivery are punctuated by negative body language, the impact of your message will be lost. Remember, you never get a second chance to make a good first impression!

The personal body language or non-verbal element of your communication must be positive to make a good impression. The factors which comprise this component of the message you send include these three groups:

Voice:
  Pace of speech
  Clarity
  Pitch
  Volume
  Tone
  Expressiveness

Body Language

Your Body
   Appearance
   Facial expression
   Eye contact
   Your posture
   The way you move
   The gestures you make

Relationship to others
   Use of touch
   Sensitivity to, and use of, personal space

Many people acknowledge that women are more intuitive than men. When we call someone intuitive, we are referring to their ability to read another person's non-verbal cues and to compare these cues with verbal signals. Women are particularly good at this. When we say that we have a hunch or 'gut feeling' that someone is not telling the truth, we really mean that their body language and their spoken words do not match. This is also what speakers often call audience awareness or rapport. Women are generally more perceptive than men and this fact has given rise to what is commonly referred to as women's intuition. Women seem to have an innate ability to pick up and interpret non-verbal cues, as well as having an eye for small details. This is why few males can lie to their partners and get away with it, and why, conversely, a woman can pull the wool over the man's eyes without him realising it! This female intuition is particularly evident in women who have raised children. For the first few years, the mother relies heavily on the non-verbal exchanges to communicate with the child and this is believed to be the reason why women often become more perceptive negotiators than men.

You must use body language consciously and deliberately. Research has shown that when the verbal and non-verbal message are in conflict, the audience will believe the non-verbal message. I attended a presentation recently, where the saleswoman was extolling the virtues of a particular computer system. When it came to question time, it was evident from her body language that she was uneasy about answering questions. After asking for questions in a monotone, she proceeded to tidy up the papers on the table in front of her whilst looking longingly at the door, obviously praying for a quick exit! The audience picked up on these cues, and responded in similar vein. They asked a few half-hearted questions which were answered with little enthusiasm, and the presentation ended on a low note.

EYE CONTACT AND FACIAL EXPRESSION

Throughout history we have been preoccupied with the eyes and their effect on human behaviour. In certain light conditions, the pupils will dilate or contract as a person's attitude and mood change from positive to negative and vice versa. When someone becomes excited, their pupils dilate to up to four times their normal size. Conversely, an angry or negative mood can contract them to what are often described as 'beady little eyes'. It is only when you are eye-to-eye with another person that a good basis for communication can be established. Bear in mind that you are communicating with people; the audience is made up of individuals. Make eye contact with each of those individuals, but not in a pattern, and not jerkily. Remember, the longer you hold your gaze on individuals, the more sincere you seem to be. Do not stare them out, though! And do not favour some more than others.

Unless the message is meant to be serious, look pleasant; smile when you can. Cultivate a pleasant and positive expression. But keep it in check. Smile at individuals when you answer a question, or make reference to them. It's a psychological fact that facial expressions alter emotions and that in time we grow in tune with our most usual expression. So, if you confront your audience with a face like a wet weekend, sooner or later that's how you're going to feel!

'It's not just what you do that counts, it's how you do it', says Professor Paul Ekman. He's found three basic types of smile:

- **The Felt Smile**
  This is the natural smile, a genuine expression of a positive emotion, which usually lasts between two and four seconds. It's unique in that it uses the orbicularis oculi muscle around the eye, as well as the zygotic major muscle (the muscle which turns the corners of the mouth upwards). In other words, when someone is smiling because she means it, you can see it in her eyes.

- **The False Smile**
  As used by failed Miss World contestants. It tends to be more lopsided than the real variety, and to last a second or two longer. And it *never* reaches the eyes.

- **The Miserable Smile**
  Usually used when someone is trying to put a brave face on things, this is the most lopsided of them all.

But a smile doesn't have to be genuine to make you feel better. In an American study, a group of actors were asked to play-act various expressions while their heart rate, blood pressure and skin temperature were monitored. In every case, these functions all calmed down when the actors were smiling. Doctors believe smiling produces hormones which have a positive influence on body functions. Looking happy can actually pick you up!

PHYSICAL PRESENCE

When an actress walks onto the stage, her presence commands attention even before she opens her mouth to speak: the actress has mastered the ability to project herself. This stage presence has a great deal to do with deportment, how she holds herself, and her ability to project her image to an audience as someone totally self-controlled. The qualities you want to project in your business presentations are those of confidence, authority and conviction.

Posture

Learn to stand tall with your head and chin up, your rib cage high, your stomach tucked in. When you are standing, push your head up as high as you can – feel it stretching. Then let your shoulders slump, as if you were trying to lift a heavy object from the floor. Keep your feet slightly apart with the weight evenly distributed.

Gestures and movements

Erratic movements signal bad news to the audience; the message is that you are tense, nervous and worried. Such an attitude in turn evokes a negative response: uncertainty and distrust. In presentations, a relaxed, responsive and smooth series of movements helps the audience to relax. It will also be easier for you to listen creatively, to smile and gesture as appropriate. Remember, a static pose held for more than a few minutes can be boring for your audience; too much movement and it is distracting. Vary your movement and check that it is purposeful, for example, a gesture for emphasis, a move to change a slide, or write on the flipchart.

Body Language

Hands

What not to do with them:

- clutch back of chair, table, lectern. This says 'My notes are here and I'm not moving from this spot'.
- fiddle with keys, loose change, jewellery, hair, face, notes.
- Adopt any static pose for too long.

Some favourite poses:

The fig-leaf position: hands clasped in front of the body.

The Duke of Edinburgh: hands clasped behind back.

The frustrated orchestra conductor: waves pen, pointer in the air.

The housewife: tidies up paper, notes in front of her.

The lover: let's leave him until later!

Most presenters have a favourite pose, such as with hands loosely held in front. Find out which hand movements you feel are natural and comfortable for you. If possible, and if it is a small group, try and get near to your audience, but be aware of their personal space. Standing *too* close can make them feel uncomfortable.

CONTROLLING NERVES

> **'The human brain starts the moment you are born and never stops until you stand up to speak in public.'**
> *Sir George Jessel*

If you are to overcome the phobia of public speaking, it is essential to get to the root of it. Problems vary from person to person but are mostly symptomised by a sense of vulnerability, a condition familiar to many women. The fear of making a fool of yourself or forgetting what you were going to say produces all kinds of symptoms. The most common symptoms reported by women presenters are:

rapid speech
hand, leg and knee shake
shallow breathing
drying up and losing the flow
static posture
negative body language, e.g. poor eye contact
blotchiness on face and neck
sweaty palms
palpitations and feelings of panic
nausea.

Most people who give presentations have experienced some, if not all, of the above symptoms at one time or another. Experienced presenters also are nervous when they speak in public, but experience has taught them how to control and harness their nervous energy. On a recent chat show a well-known actor was discussing his latest film. The presenter asked him if he was nervous whilst making it. He replied, 'Not only was I nervous, but I actually saw what adrenalin looked like!' This sounds a bit drastic, but two of the women in the survey (see Ch. 11) said that they have actually been physically sick before making a presentation.

Professionals often have a favourite method of conquering stage fright. Dorothy Sarnoff, former actress and now a speech and image consultant, recommends the Sarnoff Squeeze. Besides preventing fear, this method reduces negative feelings like anger, anxiety, depression and fatigue; it also generates energy. Her book *Never Be Nervous Again* describes how she has taught her method in many strange places, including a demonstration to

Body Language

former UN Ambassador Jeanne Kirkpatrick during lunch in a restaurant. She also claims to have taught it in ladies' rooms, in taxicabs, and at dinner parties!

Here is how to do it:

> Sit in a straight-back chair. Carry your rib cage high, but not in a ramrod-straight military position. Incline slightly forward.

> Now put your hands together just in front of your chest, your elbows akimbo, your fingertips pointing upward, and push so that you feel an isometric opposing force in the heels of your palms and under your arms.

> Say 'ssss', like a hiss. As you're exhaling the sound, contract the muscles in the vital triangle as though you were rowing a boat against a current, pulling the oars back. The vital triangle should feel like a tightening corset.

> Relax the muscles at the end of your exhalation, then inhale gently.

Contracting those muscles prevents the production of noradrenaline and epinephrine, the fear-producing chemicals in your system. So, when you want to shake off nervousness, sit with your vital triangle contracted, your lips slightly parted and release your breath over your lower teeth on a silent hiss. You can do this anywhere.

Flopsy bunny

We often yawn when feeling stressed or nervous. This exhalation of breath is useful to control nerves and calm oneself (observe the dedicated smoker). I first encountered the following exercise some years ago when I attended a stress management workshop. There was a group of managers, most of whom were overweight and dressed in an assortment of leotards and tracksuits. The course leader, of the Joyce Grenfell school, shouted 'Now then, boys and girls – let's do the flopsy bunny!' Well, if the flopsy bunny works, here it is:

- Exhale, bending over your stomach.
- Now stand straight and slowly breathe in deeply through your mouth.
- Repeat twice.

You should feel relaxed and energised after this. Be careful not to extend this, because too much oxygen may make you dizzy.

Deep breathing

This is one of the simplest exercises which can be done anywhere. Try it in the period before you give your presentation:

- Draw a good deep breath into the stomach.
- Release air slowly, counting to ten out loud.
- Continue until you build up a rhythm.

When you feel nervous, keep in mind that:

- Fear is a normal experience. The fact that you are afraid indicates that you are like most other people.
- Fears are not well founded: speakers do not die while speaking, or even faint. Audiences usually receive them sympathetically.
- Unless you are presenting a thesis to which the audience seriously objects, your audience want you to succeed.

- Presenters who are well prepared almost always give creditable performances.

- Nervousness tends to disappear with added experience.

- Presenters seldom look as frightened as they feel. Audiences rarely see a speaker's knees tremble or her face flush.

- The tension you feel at the beginning of your presentation is helpful. Presenters who no longer find an audience stimulating are likely to be dull. Use the nervous energy to sharpen your delivery and concentrate on getting your points across.

In conclusion, follow these guidelines to help you overcome your fear:

- Tell a story from your personal experience. Your audience are interested in you. For many, the most relaxing way to begin any presentation is to explain how you came to be involved with your topic.

- Think about relaxing your audience. Put your audience at ease.

- Think positive: concentrate on being yourself, rather than thinking about how nervous you feel. Change your tension into enthusiasm for your subject. Visualise yourself doing a great job.

APPEARANCE

We have seen that, initially, most of the message you communicate comes from appearance and body language; what you wear speaks louder than words. Psychologist Jane Firbank states that 'the conditioning of women to

Presenting For Women in Business

Is your appearance PMA?

value themselves on the basis of appearance starts at an early age. People compliment boys for their achievements. They compliment girls for being good and pretty!' But the pressures on women to look good have become even greater in recent years. 'A hundred years ago you would judge your appearance in comparison with the other women you had seen', says Firbank. 'Now every woman can be judged against the best in the world. Staring out from the cover of every glossy magazine is an immaculately groomed, perfectly made-up face, while the fashion pages and ads inside show flawless, bronzed size 8 bodies. Little wonder that 90 per cent of women regard themselves as overweight and that most say they would rather lose 10–15 lbs than any other goal.' (Incidentally, did you know that over 55 per cent of British women wear a dress size of 14 and over?)

When reviewing your appearance, consider how you will be perceived by your audience. Your appearance should be appropriate to you, your position and your message. Sally, a management accountant, firmly believes that when giving presentations, first impressions count most – and if you look deadly, you're dead. 'It is essential to look as good as you can,' says Sally. 'I have to take a pride in myself because I deal with clients. To them I *am* the company I represent.'

Some years ago, when seeking a bank loan to launch The Body Shop, Anita Roddick was unsuccessful; when she returned at a later date, having swopped her jeans and tee-shirt for a smart business suit, she was successful!

The following are some suggestions to take into account when planning your personal appearance:

Colour
The colour you wear creates one of the strongest body signals. Take care with colour. Texture, designs and colouring must relate to each other. Dark colours tend to be more formal and impressive; light colours tend to be more informal and friendly. Put on pink and the message

Presenting For Women in Business

that comes across is that you are soft and feminine – and a possible pushover?

One of the popular glossy magazines claims that when it comes to body language, red speaks volumes about the stylish, spirited woman of today; red is never out of the fashion spotlight for long. However, in the 1980s black was dominant, adopted by career-minded women as a safety cloak for their femininity. Fashion designers declare that red is the 'new black'. Red makes a statement, invites attention and makes an impression in business. Wear red by all means if you look good in it and it compliments your colouring; if not, avoid it. The secret of looking well groomed is to wear the colours that look good on you and that you feel good wearing. Don't wear a colour or style just because it's in fashion!

- Avoid new clothes straight from the packaging. It is obvious that they are not comfortable yet.

- Check that what is underneath will not be revealed. Avoid lumps and lines. Beware – you could be standing against bright light!

- Shoes should be clean, and avoid those wear marks at the heel from driving. Keep a spare pair of shoes in the car specifically for that purpose.

- Ensure that your clothes are properly adjusted, that zips and buttons are secured.

Many women complain about the crumpling effect on blouses and clothes in general caused by wearing a seat belt. Hilary, a PR executive, often has to travel long distances by car to attend client presentations: 'I always travel in casual clothes to the venue,' says Hilary. 'I allow extra travelling time, and carry my business clothes in a suit carrier. That way, I can arrive, freshen up and change. I feel more confident knowing that I look good!'

Here are some of the responses regarding dress and appearance given by women in the questionnaires.

Body Language

Dress and Appearance

Be happy with your appearance.

Dress must be appropriate, tidy and professional, i.e. no bare legs, high heels, short skirts, or low-cut blouses. These will only distract (the male) and irritate (the female) audience.

To be regarded professionally, you have to look the part. You want the audience to concentrate on the content of your presentation and not your appearance. (A suit and blouse/shirt always go down well.)

The way you look makes the first, most important impression and affects how you yourself feel.

If you are dressed suitably and comfortably, it will increase your confidence level.

Do not wear provocative clothes, which will take attention away from the subject you are presenting.

Wrong choice of clothes will kill the content.

Dress elegantly not provocatively.

Dress comfortably and for *yourself*.

Dress = power.

Clothes should always be appropriate for the occasion.

Look professional and stylish without appearing intimidating. This ensures that the audience take you seriously. Success is what it is all about and if you appear to be successful, you are half-way there.

Wear a high neckline and reasonable skirt length. You are the object of attention throughout your presentation; don't distract, just impress.

Look nice, so your audience doesn't mind having to look at you.

Presenting For Women in Business

Dress appropriately. Image is important – confident dressing helps project confidence.

Present a smart, neat and professional image so that people expect to hear something smart and professional.

Dress well and with authority.

It may be unfair, but unfortunately it's true, that if you dress like a bimbo, then you will be treated as a bimbo. (The observation of one manager on attending a presentation where the female presenter was dressed in very high heels and extremely short skirt.)

You should look well turned out, clean, tidy and above all professional. A suit is always smart, nothing flashy. Simple elegance is the thing to aim for – and no scuffed shoes!

Wear simple, well-cut clothes in subdued colours.

Wear comfortable clothes and shoes – fiddling is distracting and uncertainty about appearance increases nervousness.

Take care with your appearance. Don't let your appearance detract from your message. Men tend to be more critical about dress and habits than women.

Your appearance should suit the tone of the presentation. Formal or informal, but always smart and professional.

If you don't make a good first impression, you won't be asked back for a second!

Dress as smartly as you can to give yourself a confidence boost.

Develop your own personal style, smart but individual.

Body Language

I know that if I feel good by, for example, wearing smart clothes, I feel psychologically better prepared, and I think the audience's confidence level is raised.

Pay attention to your non-verbal as well as to your verbal messages, in particular your appearance, stance and gestures.

Be comfortable, smart and streamlined (no unsightly bulges or obvious outlines).

Look businesslike, neat and tidy, nothing fussy.

FEEDBACK

> 'O wad some pow'r the giftie gi'e us
> To see ourselves as ithers see us
> It wad frae mony a blunder free us
> An' foolish notion'.
> *Robert Burns*

Feedback is an essential ingredient of good communication. Just as your audience will be reading your signals, you will be reading theirs!

The following is a Body Language checklist for large group presentations:

Presentation

Always stand to make a presentation – command your audience and create a presence.

Always face the audience. Avoid looking at visual aids or out of the window.

Don't hide behind a high lectern. Come out and let them see your body. Above all, don't hide your chest area.

Presenting For Women in Business

Get close to your audience if you can. Staying away suggests you are frightened. Come down from your position; reach out and get them to join with you.

Hold yourself well. Make sure your stance is good and balanced. Never twist, slump or lean. Stand up, and look out!

Let the natural feelings in your body come out. Use your gestures and movements to add a dimension to your words.

Meeting clients – one-to-one

Sit as close as client allows at 90°–120° orientation. This reduces threat of appearing dominant or over pally.

Turn at least head and shoulders directly to client.

Lean towards client.

Legs crossed at start, uncross them as you become comfortable.

Hands loosely held in lap.

Tilt head when listening.

Take notes.

'Match' their body language as appropriate.

What to look for

Think of people like flowers: closed, and they are defensive, negative; open, and they are warm, receptive.

Head down = negative. Head comes up = interested. Head to the side, perhaps with a finger vertical up to the cheekbone = evaluating, deeply interested.

If you are slow, boring, covering known ground, then the audience gets impatient, tapping, twitching, and fiddling with things.

If they have had enough, they turn to something else, such as a diary or another paper. They look at their watch or the clock; they even look longingly at the door!

If they are bored, they become lethargic, stop looking at you and put their heads down or in their hands, eyes half-shut.

People move all the time. Look for feedback, and match how you work to how they react. Unless you must stick to a script, be driven by the audience, not by your notes. If the audience turns off, you waste your time and theirs.

SUMMARY

Appearance and body language are important elements to consider if you wish to create a positive and professional image. The professional woman presenter should not be interested in stereotypes. Firbank states that 'women need to adopt different values, and women are not in that particular race anymore!' We do, however, need to make the very best of what we have. 'I don't think people worry too much about how good-looking we are, as long as we are neat and tidy,' says Jane, a stewardess with British Airways. 'BA tends to go for people who appear pleasing, open and who smile', she adds.

Vidal Sassoon, much in demand for his views on health and beauty, claims that hair is not the most important source of a woman's beauty, nor her face or figure. Femininity is due to more subtle things, like body language, eyes and voice. You can do something with these without having physical attributes. Professor D.B. Bromley, who has written a book on human ageing, says, 'You have nothing to lose if you have the basic skills of smiling, making eye contact, and good use of gestures, posture and general body language... Our view of a person's attractiveness is largely based on these'.

Presenting For Women in Business

Age and time can improve one's social skills and can actually render a person a lot *more* attractive. It's time for us all to kiss goodbye to the immature and all-too-fleeting attraction of a pretty face, and say hello again to womanhood!

Body Language

What to Wear on Television – the basic 'Do's' and 'Don'ts'

Select something from your wardrobe that reflects your professional image and with which you are comfortable.

Don't wear apparel with lumpy textures, such as bulky tweeds, or novelty weaves that might expand or exaggerate on camera.

Rely on familiar fashion classics rather than extreme high fashion or trendy garments that might divert attention.

Avoid clothes such as recreational sportswear or evening wear, when they do not complement your normal occupational role.

Choose apparel with subdued colours that do not overpower your natural skin-tone.

Don't wear strongly patterned or shiny fabrics which appear to quiver on television.

Avoid colours that blend into those of the studio set and lighting conditions. If possible, bring along an optional outfit to avoid this.

Avoid curiosities in jewellery or accessories that might divert attention from your message.

Choose small accessories (earrings for women, cuff links for men) which enhance your apparel.

Don't wear accessories that are large, move too much, glare, or make a noise.

Keep your hairstyle simple, making sure it does not obscure your face from different camera angles.

Don't use exaggerated make-up. Be guided by the station make-up artist or on-camera station personnel.

When possible, call the station in advance for guidance on the colour and tonality of your on-air apparel.

Presenting For Women in Business

Appearance and Body Language Checklist

> Dress smartly and be well groomed – remember your PMA. Your dress should be appropriate to your Position, your Message and your Audience.
>
> 'Upright' posture (i.e. head up, shoulders back, chest out, stomach in, back straight).
>
> Stand up.
>
> Get as close to the audience as possible.
>
> Make eye contact with as many people as possible.
>
> Smile occasionally – but not at individuals, unless specifically referring to them.
>
> Project voice and facial expression; put variety into both.
>
> More gestures and movement than usual, but keep purposeful.
>
> Relax and enjoy yourself.

Liz Forgan, Director of Programmes for Channel 4, has been described as the complete opposite of the designer-clad image of the 'successful female executive'. In fact, she's regularly described as 'headmistressy'. There is a certain sense of mischief about the way she looks. She says, 'The secret, I've noticed, is to look respectable, as if you're chairwoman of the WI, and you can get away with all manner of bad behaviour and radical views. If you look like a revolutionary, people jump on you'.

7
Visual Aids

'A picture paints a thousand words –
but only if it's a good one!'

D. Leeds

Are visual aids necessary in business presentations? Most presentations are enhanced by the use of visuals. However, in motivational presentations, visuals are superfluous. Used for this purpose, they arrest the spontaneity and flow. It is estimated that the average manager spends 50 per cent of her time in meetings and presentations. By using good visual aids, you can produce the greatest amount of communication in the shortest amount of management time.

Visuals can:

- encourage logical thought in your audience (also in the presenter.) For example, overheads can help break up the spoken information. They can be introduced to summarise key sections and act as a focus.
- if well designed, supplement the presentation; invite co-operation, illustrate relationships, challenge; consolidate.
- add impact and interest.
- make it easier and faster for you to convey messages which may not be understood unless they are both seen and heard simultaneously. This is especially

Presenting For Women in Business

Visual aids

Visual Aids

helpful when introducing a new concept or showing the application of ideas.

The more of the audience's senses you use, the more effectively you communicate. Visuals also increase your listeners' retention; verbalised messages can easily be either misinterpreted or forgotten, but visual aids used correctly can help increase retention.

For visual aids to benefit you, they must be effectively prepared and handled. Make sure that they clarify, not confuse, information. Good visual aids are:

- legible
- appropriate
- up-to-date
- well designed
- accurate
- realistic
- manageable
- meaningful and necessary.

Any visual aid that fails to meet these requirements should be avoided – your presentation will be better without any aids at all than with ones that are ineffective. If you must apologise for a visual aid, you should not be using it.

Some general guidelines for handling visual aids:

Before presenting them, brief your audience on the material each will cover.

Explain the key points during the presentation.

Repeat the key points after the presentation.

Handle them smoothly.

Presenting For Women in Business

Present them in their most effective sequence.

Make sure that everyone can see them clearly, that neither you nor the equipment is in the way.

Consider these factors when selecting visual aids:

the type of presentation being given

the location and the facilities available

preparation time available

cost of the visual aids

the specific audience and your objectives.

OVERHEAD SLIDES

One of the most popular visual aids is overhead slides, or OHPs. In addition to being quick and inexpensive to make, overheads provide:

- **Illumination**
  The large projection area, usually 10 × 10 inches, permits a lot of light to reach the screen. As a result, you can use it with a fairly large number of people. Overheads can also be used in a fully lighted room.
- **Speaker control**
  Not only can the group see the slides, but so can you. This offers you better control of the group and more eye contact. You will be able to be more attentive to their reactions.
- **Speaker identification**
  Overhead slides are the part of your presentation that illustrates what you are saying. You also have the flexibility to manipulate your slides; you can turn the projector off entirely to make a verbal point, can reveal

material on the slide a little at a time, or can point to specific words.

- **Facilitation**
  Overhead projectors are easy to use. The new models are quiet enough to offer little distraction.

The following are some common faults:

Comprehensive
Too *much* detail; remember that a slide is only part of what you are asking the audience to take in – you supply the other part with what you say over it. You can always say, 'This, of course, is only a broad outline of the system', and so on. Indeed, the best slides are not sufficient on their own; they need the presenter's words to make them properly intelligible. If they don't, the audience is liable to stop listening to her and start working out the information on the slide.

Complex
Many slides are such a mass of boxes and arrows that you might as well put up a maze. The solution is usually to break them down into a sequence of successive slides; keep them simple.

Crowded
Too much information; excessive information on the slide, even if reasonably simple, makes it impossible for the back half of the audience to see important detail. If in any doubt, get someone who has never seen the slides before to sit at the furthest audience distance in the room and be honest. Again, a sequence of slides can work here.

Colour
Colour can bring pleasant variations to your slides and is more interesting than black outlines on clear slides. When you start thinking in terms of a colour range, you begin to find ways in which colour keys and codes can be used to help the audience's comprehension by giving additional information. There are many colour choices

available, but select carefully. Your visuals should not look like rainbows.

Format
Although both vertical and horizontal formats are acceptable, the horizontal (often referred to as landscape) format is usually considered best for audience viewing. Remember that titles should generally be at the top of the transparency, and information should be in the upper two thirds for better visibility. Have a focal point, i.e. the point of interest, in the centre of the transparency.

OVERHEAD SLIDE TECHNIQUES

Once the slide has made its point, it should be removed, unless there is a positive reason for keeping it there; otherwise, it becomes a distraction. Be aware that often when various companies make a succession of presentations, a company will leave up a slide with the company logo when their speaker leaves. The next speaker may then present with the competitive logo showing.

- **Overlays** are overheads designed to be used on top of one another. Develop ideas one at a time, making sure the audience understands each overlay before you add the next. Frame your first slide, then tape the subsequent overlays of the same size alongside one edge of the first frame. Notes and key words can then be written on the frames.

- **Negative overheads** are prepared with black instead of clear backgrounds and your reversed graphics will then project as clear or colour. A variation of this technique can be done by covering up your graphics with tape and 'turning' words on and off almost electrically on a single transparency.

- **Reveal:** if you have an explanation to unfold, or a complex diagram to show, reveal it piece by piece.

Visual Aids

- **Place a pointer** (pen or pencil will do) on the portion of your slide to which you want to draw attention.

- **Turn the projector on and off**, depending on whether you want the spotlight on yourself or to share it with a slide.

- **Use dual projectors,** one in each corner; alternate them to create a faster pace for effect. Or keep your agenda or logo on one and use the other.

- **Pre-prepare** overheads. In a formal presentation, never write on them. Keep this for informal discussion groups.

- **Place** your overhead on the projector before switching on.

- **Be selective:** a few good visuals are often better than many. Too many visuals may dilute the key points. The number of visuals may depend on how graphic your information is and to some degree on how long you plan to talk. There have been effective presentations with just one visual.

Transparencies of printed information from books and magazines will usually not be large enough to be legible when they are projected. So be careful to select material which has printing at least as large as the Orator 10 font.

Obtaining OHPs

Producing OHPs is relatively easy and cheap. Copy bureaux can design and prepare them very quickly. Many companies have graphics terminals and plotters available in-house. This computer hardware and software makes it easy to prepare slides. With, for example, 'SLIDE' you enter your text and a few simple specifications into a menu displayed on the terminal's screen. The specifications describe how you want your text drawn by the plotter (what type font and size you want, whether or not you want the text centred, what colour pen you want used, and so on). You can have one set of specifications apply to the entire slide or you can change any of them from one text line to another.

35mm SLIDES

These are not as flexible as overhead slides. They are used in a darkened room which makes it difficult to establish eye contact with the audience. If you want feedback, you will probably be beside the screen, and can see it from the corner of your eye without looking directly at it. If it is a large room, with the screen behind and above you, put a folding mirror on the lectern so that you can see the image of the slide.

It is also a good idea to arrange for a spotlight to shine on you during the showing. This means that the audience can see you and you can also read your notes. Some lecterns have in-built lamps. Place the screen against the centre wall with the projector in front of it.

Check that the slides are placed in the carousel the right way round. To do this:

- Hold up the slide to the projector light so that you can read it.
- Place the slide in the carousel upside down, so that the top of the slide enters first.
- Number each slide.
- Check the slides are in order and practise with the remote control.

Check the projector for the following:

- focus
- loading mechanism

Visual Aids

- bright enough light
- spare bulb.

The best person to operate the projector is the presenter, by using the remote push-button control. If you have someone else operating it, it is doubly important for you to rehearse together; you must have confidence in the projectionist. Work out any codes to exchange information. Cueing can best be done using the script with cue keywords.

VIDEO AND FILM

Videos are often used to 'kick off' sales presentations. The advantage of this is that the material shown lays the foundation for the presentation and the audience starts from the same knowledge base. Videos and films also provide a pleasant change of pace for your lengthier presentations.

FLIPCHARTS

The flipchart is a useful aid, but its use is limited to small groups of up to about thirty people. It is an excellent aid for discussion and brain-storming sessions.

Stand to one side of the chart stand, on the right if you're right-handed and on the left if you are left-handed. To check correct positioning, try this. Grasp the edge of the chart with your left hand and move it slightly back to your right. Your arm should now be fully extended. Think of your gripping arm as a hinge. This means that you will cover part of the board as you write. By swinging back on the 'hinge', you can reveal what you have written to the people on your right.

Presenting For Women in Business

Don't let the 'transparent lover' take over. This presenter tends to write words and draw diagrams, while you are wondering if his face is less unattractive than his back, and lovingly chats to his artwork as if it were Kim Basinger. The audience can't see through you, so minimise the time that you have your back to them. When you are using the flipchart:

- Don't talk and write at the same time.
- Use key words instead of sentences so that you cut down the writing time.
- Stand back to allow the audience to read it.
- Write in large clear lettering.

Many presenters do not like using the flipchart because they fear that their writing is not legible or that they can't write in a straight line. Practice will allay these fears. There are also many types of charts on the market which may help solve the problem, such as those with lined or graph paper.

Use the pencil technique; with this, you can prepare your flip chart in advance. Lightly sketch out your graph or diagram in pencil. At the appropriate time, you can then go over it in pen. I have seen this work very successfully in a technical presentation. The presenter built up his diagram on the flipchart to help explain a particular aspect of his computer hardware. (This technique can also work using the whiteboard.) You can use it to help with spacing and to indicate starting points for headings. It can also be used to present statistical data. The words or figures can be written in lightly and overwritten at the appropriate point in your presentation. Key words can be written at the side of the chart. Your audience won't be able to see them and they act as a memory aid for you.

Visual Aids

When preparing your flipcharts in advance, label each page. Place a tab of white sticky tape folded neatly at the left-hand edge of the sheet and labelled. As you prepare each sheet, label it and turn over to the next. Leave a blank sheet in between each one prepared (or more if required). The sheets can then be readily identified and are thus easy to locate should you wish to refer back to a previous one.

WHITEBOARD

This visual aid comes in many forms, from the flip chart size to large screen size. The larger boards are particularly useful for presentations which require a big display area, for example, technical presentations where diagrams can be built up and left on the board for reference. If you decide to use the whiteboard, remember that you must use the appropriate type of dry marker pen. If you use standard chart pens on the whiteboard you will find it difficult, if not impossible, to erase your artwork. Invest in some of the cleaning solution made specifically for this purpose. A special penholder attached to the board could help prevent mixing the different types of pens.

Whiteboards have been around for some time. Many variations are now available, for example, the copy board. This allows you to write on a dry-wipe surface, and then copy the result down to A4 size for handouts. The electronic whiteboard is a touch-sensitive whiteboard that captures a written message or drawing and transmits it down a telephone line to a compatible monitor, projector, or printer. A smaller version of this is also available. Using the same technology, the sender uses a desk-top writing/sketching tablet, either A4 or A5 in size. An optional disk storage unit allows received images to be recalled at will for later study and evaluation.

Many whiteboards also double as magnetic boards. These are often secured to a wall and can be used for maps or charts with small magnets. The pieces are held by magnets, and magnetic string can be used to link ideas and build up flow diagrams. Titles and labels can be added to build up the required effect.

DISPLAY BOARD

This can be used for an informal discussion. It can be used on a desk or table top and is useful for a one-to-one session or a small group. As you turn over each page, you know what it shows as you have the information on the reverse of the next one. It allows you to give the listener good eye contact; you can sit face to face or sideways on. The graphics displayed should be of high quality, no less than if you were presenting the information to a large group.

PROPS

Props are another way of enhancing your presentation. When used correctly they can put you more at ease, aid in making your presentation clearer and more vivid, and enable you to seize and hold attention.

The most significant guideline for using equipment or props is that you should practise using them beforehand. It is embarrassing when you expect a machine to do one thing and it does another – or nothing at all!

- Pick up your prop only when you are ready to use it.
- Hold it high enough for everyone to see it.
- Hold it so it does not hide your face.
- Talk to the audience, not to the exhibit.

Visual Aids

- Put it aside when you have finished with it.

The more visuals you use, the more practice you will need. This is particularly the case with many of the computer-based systems.

Tips on using a pointer

- Pointers should be used to make a quick visual reference on a pictorial chart or to trace the relationship of data on a graph.
- When using a pointer, keep your shoulder facing the audience. Stretch your arm out fully. Hold the pointer in the hand which is close to the screen.
- Don't play with the pointer (no frustrated orchestra conductors, please). Retract the pointer and put it down when not using it.

DEVELOPING TITLES FOR YOUR VISUAL AIDS:

Choose the type of title which best suits your need.

Subject title

This type of title is used when it is not necessary to convey a specific message but only to provide information, as in the example below:

SALES FIGURES

Thematic title

Used to tell the audience what information they should get from the data provided. For example,

Sales in 1990 were up 40% over 1989.

Assertive title
Used when you want to give the audience your opinion about what conclusion they should draw from the information given. It is often used in persuasive presentations. An example would be:

We should focus our sales effort on Scotland.

VARIETY OF VISUAL AIDS

Give some thought to the advantages and limitations of the different visual and audio aids. Choose the ones which best suit your purpose. Avoid using too many different types, which can be confusing for the audience. Limit yourself to one or two, plus a flipchart for discussion.

Vary the way you use your visuals. For example instead of a talk followed by a show every time, try to sometimes:

- Show your visual aid first before you talk.
- Build up the information.
- Show the aid and keep silent in order to let the audience absorb the image.
- Build up a picture with a succession of overheads.

Avoid writing on overhead slides. This method is only acceptable in, for example, informal departmental meetings. Ever since the introduction of visual aids, the overhead projector has maintained high popularity. The ease and economy of preparation and the portability of the machines makes it a popular item in the manager's toolkit.

Here are some examples and hints on the different types of overhead slide layout:

Visual Aids

Flowcharts

These can be used to show stages of development. You may use a flowchart to illustrate a number of steps in sequence.

Line graphs

Use the line graphs to illustrate variations over a period of time or to show relative facts; for example, if you wish to compare production figures between 1985 and 1990 for production outputs which vary over this five-year time-scale.

Pie charts

Use pie charts to show parts of a whole at any one point in time. Pie charts are designed to show total amounts and also their parts, calculated in percentage or fractional segments; for example, when illustrating expenditure in the different company areas, i.e. marketing, sales, production, advertising.

There is an excellent video on slide presentation made by Video Arts. It outlines all the do's and don'ts. In one particular scene John Cleese plays the manager who is giving his colleague advice on slide presentation. Picture the scene: the audience is assembled and the presenter puts up a pie chart, saying, 'And now you can see at a glance how your money has been spent'. Camera pans to audience who almost turn through 90 degrees trying to decipher the information. Giving feedback later, Cleese advises the presenter: 'The only person who benefited from that slide was the osteopath – my neck still gives me gip when I think of it!' The moral is to make sure that the headings on the pie chart are horizontal!

Bar graphs

Comparative information can be shown in vertical or horizontal bars, the length of the bar representing the value. Bar graphs are flexible and easy to read.

Presenting For Women in Business

COMMUNICATION WORKS Consultancy Sales
Fiscal year ending 1990

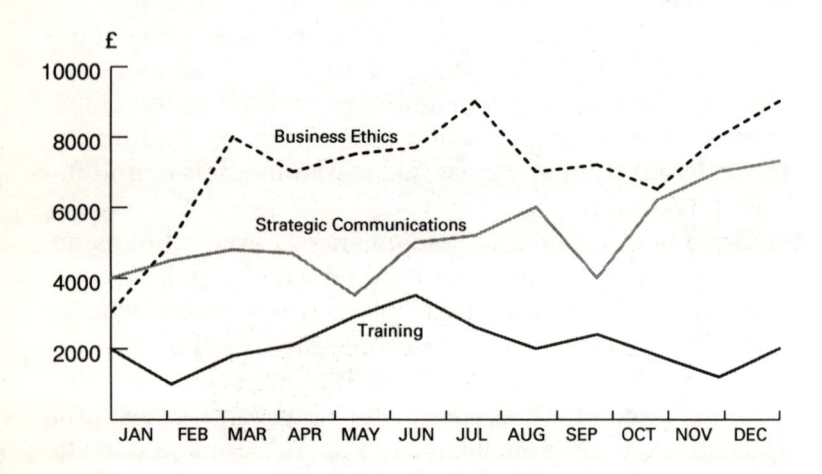

Example of line graph

Visual Aids

Sales by Area 1990

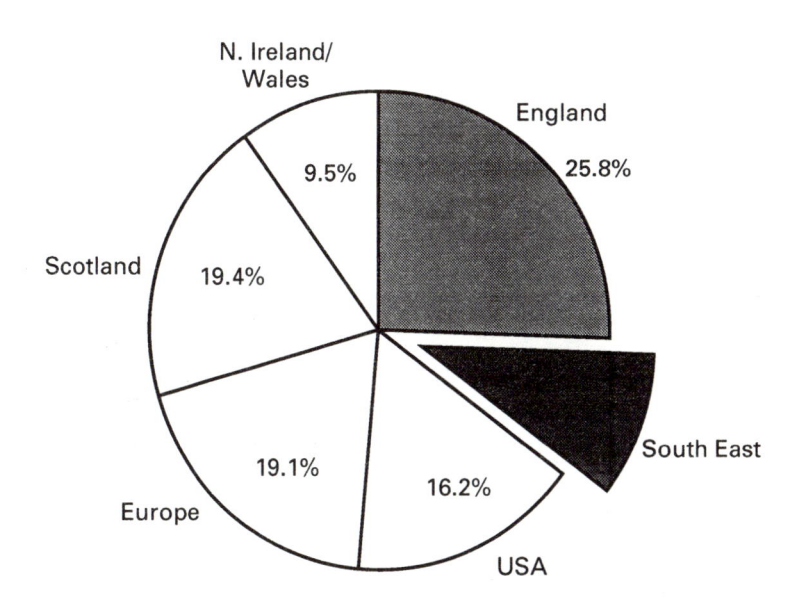

- N. Ireland/Wales 9.5%
- England 25.8%
- Scotland 19.4%
- South East
- Europe 19.1%
- USA 16.2%

Example of pie chart

Presenting For Women in Business

TAXBACK LIMITED
Sales 1986 - 1990

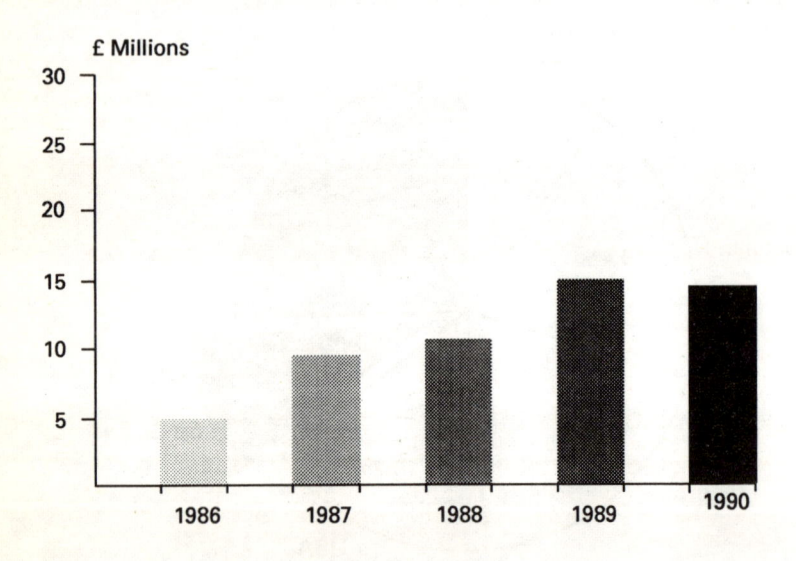

Example of bar/column chart

Visual Aids

One hundred women presenters were asked to name the *most* important **personal item** they would take to the presentation.

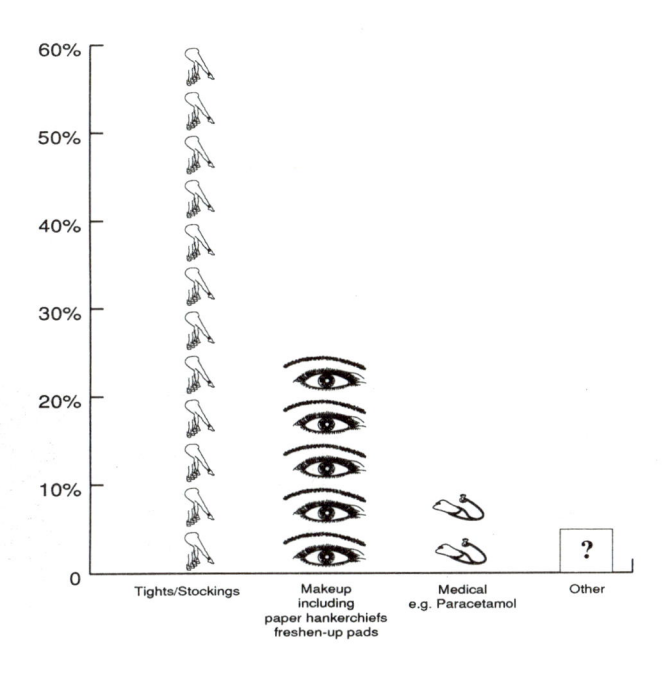

Example of pictograph

Organisation charts

These charts depict the flow and functional relationships of a business or group. The structure of the organisation will be immediately obvious: departments, titles, responsibilities. In today's fast-growing, fast-changing organisations, you may often need to show this information. Because of the fast turnover of this information, it is an area where quite often the updated chart is put through the photocopier. Frequently this will not work, because almost certainly the lettering will be too small to reproduce well on an overhead.

Pictographs

These are an interesting way of using symbols to show numerical relationships between different items or the same item; also of stimulating interest in a set of ordinary figures, by using symbols.

Creating a storyboard is a useful and quick method of checking your slides. Take a piece of paper and divide it into sections. If you are using six slides then divide the page into six and roughly draw out your slide in each section. You can then see at a glance how they fit into the scheme of things, so that you can weave your words round the slides and plan your links.

8
Questions

Four simple words that can make or break a presentation are: 'Are there any questions?' Questions invite participation. They prove that the presenter is aware of the audience. It is a good idea to ask the group to hold questions until you are finished, otherwise you risk getting sidetracked and disrupting your train of ideas. However, in certain types of presentation, for example the technical, questions will be taken during them.

LISTENING TO YOUR AUDIENCE

Here are some general guidelines for fielding questions. Dr. Albert Einstein, in giving his formula for success, $X + Y + Z =$ success, said that X represented hard work, Y represented play, and Z represented ... 'the ability to keep your mouth shut and listen'. Listening – in your case, to questions and comments from your audience – means more than hearing or even appearing attentive. It means being actively absorbed in what is being said, gaining clear insight into what is meant and what is implied and into why it was expressed in one way rather than another. Skilled listening on your part will help others to be objective and keep the discussion on target. It is also essential in encouraging participation.

As well as being the speaker, there are times in the presentation where you will take on the role of listener. Listening skills can be divided into two categories: passive; (silent, yet attentive) and active. Often we fail to pick up the messages on the emotional line, or we may pick them up, but pretend not to and ignore them. We may be so emotionally involved that we fail to hear what is said. If the gap between words and emotions (head and heart) is small, the message will be received. If, however, the gap is large, the listener will be confused.

The major processes of active listening fall into four areas:

1. Observing

Careful, non-evaluative attention and eye contact while listening automatically aids the speaker to express what he or she wishes to say. This provides a warm, accepting atmosphere for the speaker's thoughts, ideas, attitudes and values. Observation tunes the listener in to the speaker's words and the emotional 'music' which accompanies them, often revealed by facial expressions and body language.

2. Reflecting Data

This process, often referred to as 'paraphrasing', is akin to holding a mirror in front of the speaker, reflecting back phrases as you hear them. This increases clarity and lets the speaker know that you are hearing accurately.

3. Reflecting Feeling

As you become familiar with the speaker's emotions, the 'music' behind the words, reflecting them back will test your perceptions, as well as give information and feedback to the speaker about his/her feelings. This is particularly useful if words and emotions seem incongruous. Reflecting feelings provides continual testing and expressing of understanding.

4. Interpreting

Sometimes it is appropriate to interpret what the speaker is saying. However, be careful of negative reac-

Questions

tion from the speaker who may feel that you are deliberately distorting the intended message for undeclared reasons of your own. Giving attention to your questioners helps them off-load negative feelings and experiences which get in the way of clear thinking and effective action. Active listening should not be seen as a mere technique for influence; it is only useful in influencing if the listener is *genuinely* attentive and values the other individual's point of view.

At times, silent listening is the most appropriate response. Most question times will present opportunities for both passive and active listening.

BARRIERS TO GOOD LISTENING

Remember that you want to build bridges with your audience, not barriers. Here are some of the most common:

On-off listening

This unfortunate habit in listening arises from the fact that most of us think about four times as fast as the average person speaks. Thus the listener has three-quarters of a minute of spare thinking time for each listening minute. Sometimes we use this extra time to think of our own personal affairs, concerns, or interests and troubles instead of listening (going down route 350).

Open ears – closed mind listening

Sometimes we decide rather quickly that either the subject or the speaker is boring and what is said makes no sense. Often we jump to the conclusion that we can predict what he or she knows or will say and that there is no reason to listen, because we will hear nothing new if we do.

Subject centred instead of speaker centred
Often we concentrate on the problem and not the person. Detail and fact about an incident become more important than what people are saying about themselves.

Fact listening
We listen to people and try to remember the facts. As we do this, frequently the speaker has gone on to new facts and we lose them in the process.

Red-flag listening
To some of us certain words are like a red flag to a bull. When we hear them, we get upset or irritated and stop listening. These vary with individuals. However, to some words like 'feminist' or 'communist' are signals to which there is an automatic response. When this signal comes in, we tune out the speaker.

Interrupting
Question Time in Parliament is a good example. Constant interrupting does not allow the other person to speak freely. Background hubbub, noise, movement of people does not help.

KINDS OF QUESTION

What types of question should be used? Here are some examples :

With **rhetorical questions**, the presenter is not expecting a spoken answer. The presenter may hope for vocal support but not a conversation. A question or series of questions can act as a useful signpost during the presentation (e.g. 'Where does that lead us?') followed by a glimpse of the answer.

Questions

Type of question	Objective	Likely outcome in terms of type of information collected	Examples
1. Open-ended	To establish rapport at start of conversation	Facts, opinions	How are things? How was the traffic this morning?
	To open-up a particular topic	Facts, opinions, suggestions	What ideas have you got about . . .? What concerns do you have about . . .?
	To discover the feeling	Opinions	How do you feel about . . .? What's your attitude towards . . .?
2. Close	To collect specific pieces of information	Facts	How long have you worked for the company? What time did you arrive?
	To gain confirmation or otherwise of precise information	Facts, opinions in yes or no form	Do you agree? Is your title 'Sales Manager'?
3. Follow-up	To show interest and encourage person to continue talking	More facts, opinions and suggestions	Ah? So? And then?
	To increase the quantity and/or quality of information collected so far	More facts, opinions and suggestions and/or more perceptive, insightful comments	What evidence have you? Can you tell me some more about what happened? How do you mean? Why do you say that?
	To confirm your own understanding of information collected so far	Clearer restatement of earlier facts, opinions and suggestions	So how we see it is as follows? If I've heard you correctly, what you are saying is?

Three types of question

FIELDING QUESTIONS

When you ask for questions, look and sound as if you are happy to take them. Put down your notes and if it is a small group, perhaps come out into your audience. Look at the questioner and listen to the question.

Unless you know that everyone in the room has heard the question, restate it and then begin your answer. If you are asked a question which implies you were unclear in your explanation of some point, do not become defensive. Nor should you imply the listener was stupid not to understand it. Say, 'Perhaps I was not clear. What I meant to say was . . .'.

If you are asked a question which is clearly argumentative, ask the individual to expand on his concern. You might say, 'I see, that is an interesting point. Could you expand on the details?' or 'Can you tell me a little more about *why* you feel that way about . . .?' By keeping the would-be arguer talking, you frequently unearth hidden attitudes and agenda not evident in the question as posed.

If the question is fuzzy or if you are unsure what information the individual is seeking, paraphrase the question before answering it. For example, 'Bill, the way I understand the question you are asking . . .' or 'Does your question refer to the effect on customer service of . . .?'

If you don't know the answer to a question, don't bluff. Make a note of the question and tell the questioner you will get back to him or her and do so as soon as possible. If in an informal situation, you might bounce the question back to the audience. For example, if you are asked a question you can't answer, you could say, 'I'm sorry I don't know the answer to that, but perhaps someone in the audience will know?' If you are addressing a group from a variety of backgrounds, the chances are that someone in the audience will have the answer.

If the question is very technical and involves a long explanation, try and give a short answer and speak later

Questions

to the questioner, giving a fuller explanation. When you have answered the question, check that the questioner is satisfied. For example you might say, 'Does that answer your question?'

HOW TO GEAR YOUR PRESENTATION TO AUDIENCE TYPE

One of the most valuable presentation skills is 'reading' an audience. If you learn what to look and listen for, each audience will tell you how you have to sell your ideas to it. In order to do this easily, you have to identify key behaviours and select among four types of styles: relator, socialiser, director and thinker.

These styles, together with their associated behaviour, are set out overleaf. When you have counterchecked most of the characteristics, then you can use the recommendations given.

Note that some points work with both socialiser and relator, i.e. relationship orientated, and similarly some work with both director and thinker, i.e. task orientated, but there are differences in pace and forcefulness.

HANDLING OBJECTIONS

Whatever the merits of your idea, you can probably expect someone to present arguments as to why it should not be adopted. Hopefully, you will be prepared to answer these objections. Try to predict questions and have answers prepared. Play the devil's advocate with yourself: think of the strongest possible argument against your point of view and cover it in your speech. If you are refuted, introduce a telling argument in the idea's favour. Later, when a more positive tone has been built up again,

Presenting For Women in Business

Audience type	Characteristics	Hints on addressing them
Relators	relatively unassertive, warm, supportive, reliable, seen as compliant, soft-hearted, slow in action and decision, avoid risky situations, want to know others' feelings, people-orientated, friendly, personal, dislike interpersonal conflicts, strong counselling skills, listen actively, others feel good when close to a relator	Show an interest in them. Ask questions at the beginning (who are you, your company? etc.). Share personal data, stories, feelings and opinions. Move slowly, keep eye contact, be relaxed.
Socialisers	creative, think quickly 'on their feet', entertainers, seek approval, persuasive, fast pace, not concerned with details, facts, spontaneous, animated, intuitive, lively, dreamers, ideas, manipulative, impetuous, excitable.	Focus on opinions, ideas, dreams, support them with stories, animation. Move at fast, entertaining pace. Motivating presentations best received. Surprise them.

How to gear your presentation to audience type

Questions

Audience type	Characteristics	Hints on addressing them
Directors	firmness in relationship, productivity goals, bottom-line results, stubborn, take care of others/situations, decisive in actions/decisions, extremely fast pace, high achievers, good administrators, make things happen, do many things at a time	Focus on goals, facts and graphics. Audience want to gain, to be edified. Maintain fast pace. Avoid long stories, be brief, concise. Use big pictures, avoid detail and be organised. Stress the rewards. Get to the point quickly. Use assertive, powerful gestures. Show you are a competent professional.
Thinkers	prefer a structure, sceptical, great problem solvers, poor decision makers, procrastinate decisions, persistent, systematic, may be aloof, critical, need to be right, rely on dates/details, cautious in decision-making, work slowly	Support their organised approach. Establish credibility (your qualifications). Go into details, slower pace. Facts, charts, graphs, statistics are welcomed.

How to gear your presentation to audience type (contd.)

you can refer back to the argument and neutralise it further with a few positive statements. Avoid a controversial attitude at all costs. An argumentative or defensive approach creates the impression that you are not quite sold on your own idea.

In general, you should listen, not be defensive and acknowledge the objecter's point of view. ('I never thought of it like that; thank you for your thought.') When objections to your ideas are raised, you can turn them to your own advantage if you encourage the one who raised the objections to expand and elaborate. Frequently, the more one talks, the weaker the objections become. Even when the objection is irrelevant, you should stay calm. Careful listening helps you to determine whether the objection has any relevant bearing on your idea, or whether the intention is simply to reduce your stature.

Another ploy is to ask questions with which the person who raised the objection has to agree. Where applicable, a series of such questions invariably shrivels the objection and terminates in a sound conclusion with which the objecter is forced to agree. This technique, of course, requires skill and much thought beforehand.

Try not to reject objections or suggestions that would improve your idea. Even if somebody suggests something that, in your mind, would add nothing significant to your ideas, do not reject it on the spot. After you have presented your idea, arrange for a break followed, if possible, by a discussion period. The brief break will enable listeners to sort through various impressions and questions that occurred to them. During the final discussion period you should sum up the salient points of your ideas, i.e. the anticipated benefits and advantages, the need that exists or can be created for the idea, the reasons for immediate implementation of the idea.

It is particularly important to gain the enthusiasm of those who will develop and execute your idea. If your associates and subordinates, as well as your superiors, are not convinced of your ideas's value, it may fail.

Questions

HANDLING PROBLEM BEHAVIOUR

In every group, whether it be a committee meeting, a sales presentation or a special task force in marketing, there will be some behaviour which is not productive. Some examples are:

Blocking
Any action which interferes with the progress of the group. Examples of this include deliberately getting off the topic; recounting personal experiences which are irrelevant to the topic; rejecting the ideas of others; and taking a negative approach, insisting that nothing can be done. (Example: 'We tried that before and it didn't solve the problem.')

Aggression
Occurs when a member blames others for his or her own mistakes. Showing hostility to individuals or groups (company), attacking motives of others. Deflating self-image of others. (Example: 'On the face of it, your prices look good. But you don't tell the customer that a service contract is not included!')

Withdrawing
Opposite of aggression. People withdraw from the group by exhibiting such behaviour as day-dreaming, and by other acts of non-participation, such as doodling, gazing out of the window.

Seeking Status
Drawing attention by boasting, talking in an aggressive manner, distracting dress or mannerisms. (Example: 'At . . . we always do it this way.')

Dominating
Attempting to take over by excessive talking, 'pulling rank'.

Special Pleading
Going 'all out' to get a point across. Often this person will have hidden motives or hobby horses. (Example: 'All the managers in my division', the 'average woman manager'.) These are often used to cloud the issue and to support their point of view.

Distracting
Diverting attention from the task in hand. A distracting person very often comes late, interrupts others, gets off the topic. Generally non-productive behaviour.

Manipulating
Attempting to control the group by pulling strings or rank. Frequently they resort to blatant flattery (often goes on backstage). This person tends to divide the group into cliques.

Confession
Using the group for personal catharsis. The 'confessor' seeks sympathy or pity for personal mistakes, feelings, or beliefs irrelevant to the group task. (Heard recently at a presentation: 'I don't know why I have been asked to give this presentation – my background's in marketing not personnel.')

Rationalising
Explaining failure or inadequacy by finding some unsubstantiated excuse for the failure. (Example: 'Sorry I haven't finished these slides. I've been too busy lately.')

Combinations of these behaviours may surface in your group as the following types of people:

The Know-It-Alls
To handle: ask them questions to involve them and allow them to share their experiences and knowledge.

Questions

The Shy Guys
To handle: ask them open-ended questions. Reinforce any participation with a warm 'thank you'. Quiet people may feel afraid or insecure in a large group. Perhaps talk to them during the break; they need reassurance.

The Monopolisers
To handle: ask someone else, 'What do you think?' or say to the monopoliser, 'Let's hear someone else's opinion.' You could use body language to ignore them – stand in front of them and don't give them eye contact.

The Nitpickers
To handle: give their detailed questions back to them to answer, or to the group. For example, listen to the question and then put it to the group, saying 'How do others here handle that situation?'

The Machos
To handle: draw attention to them. Ask them to repeat their comments to everyone. Politely remind them of time limitations. For example, 'We only have ten minutes until we finish. Perhaps we could talk about this at coffee break.'

The Attackers
To handle: recognise the attack. Don't take it personally or be defensive. Humour often works here.

Remember that the audience will also recognise these behaviour patterns as well as you.

Checklist for handling the audience

- Welcome audience questions and they will welcome your answers.

Presenting For Women in Business

- Use open questions to discover, and closed questions to control.
- Always check back.
- Listen, observe, analyse and respond accordingly.
- Never be defensive.
- Make your audience work for you.
- Keep them on your side.

'Check that you don't obscure the screen.'

9
Set Up and Rehearsal

SET UP

- Set up all the equipment that you will use and check everything – leave nothing to chance.

- Familiarise yourself with operating the equipment – test your slides/overheads/flipchart for legibility. Check that the audience can see you and all the visual aids.

- Check your marker pens for whiteboard and flip chart are not dry.

- Check that handouts are legible and that you have sufficient numbers.

- Sit down and think through the presentation, then compile a 'What if . . .' list. What to do if:

    the light fails, or
    the microphone fails, or
    the projector bulb blows etc.

- Construct an emergency toolkit: torch (often useful), thin pliers, razor blade, fuses, sellotape. If in doubt about any of the equipment, for example the projector, have another one there.

- Tape down all wires with strong masking tape.

- Clear the area where you will be standing – everything neat and tidy and out of sight.

- Fix a 'modesty panel' to cover the front of your table. You can then put cases and handouts behind this and out of view of the audience.
- Take the water jug off the table and place it close to hand, but not on the table where you will place your notes. I have seen a presenter knock a jug of water all over his slides, and it is difficult to recover easily from this type of mishap.

When you are satisfied that the room is laid out to your satisfaction and that all the equipment is in position and in working order, go through the following checklist:

Layout agreed (see room layout suggestions)

Lighting adequate? Controllable – by whom? Can the room be darkened?

Ventilation/air conditioning – controllable, noisy?

Coffee breaks, lunches

Equipment – cables long enough? sufficient power points?

Flip chart pads, pens, paper, handouts.

REHEARSAL

Now it's time for a run-through, with all your equipment in place. Irrespective of how well prepared you are, a full rehearsal is essential. It ensures that you know how best to speak the script, timing can be checked and the script modified if necessary. It also allows you to move around and familiarise yourself with the presentation area. All visual aids can be incorporated into the presentation.

In your timing, make allowances for anticipated audience involvement or for stops during rehearsal for correcting mistakes.

Set Up and Rehearsal

Ask a colleague to sit in on your presentation and give you some feedback. Here is a feedback sheet which will help you identify areas of your presentation which need attention.

Presentation Critique

Opening
Did the presenter introduce him/herself?

Hook the audience attention.

Set clear objectives.

State how long the presentation will last.

Set ground rules for questions.

State an interesting title for the presentation and give a clear structure.

Make clear link into the main body.

Main Body
Was the structure followed throughout the presentation, with adequate signposting?

Did the presenter hold the interest of the audience?

Make clear link into the summary.

Reprise and Close
Did the presenter give an effective reprise?

Did the presenter tell the audience what action to take?

Thank the audience.

End on a high with a forceful statement.

Personal Presentation
Did the presenter show enthusiasm?

Presenting For Women in Business

Any excessive 'ums' and 'ahs'?

Any other distractions?

Body language.

Eye contact.

Gesture.

Voice.

Audience involvement.

Visual Aids
Were they legible?

Interesting?

Well managed?

Miscellaneous
Did the presentation fulfill the objectives set?

Did you enjoy it?

Timing.

Areas for improvement.

10
Other Types of Presentation

IMPROMPTU SPEAKING

Have you ever been in a staff meeting when your manager surprised you with the words, 'And now, . . . will stand up and speak to us for a few minutes about . . .?' This is referred to as an impromptu speech, one in which you must talk without preparation time, without notes, and entirely from recall. A terrifying situation; as you hear your name, your heart beats faster, your mind goes blank!

Thinking 'on your feet' is not as difficult as it may seem if you can master a few guidelines that also apply to a prepared speech. First, quickly formulate the general purpose of your talk. Are you going to ask for action, inform, persuade? Next, consider your listeners' objectives. Use the simple prompts, who, why, where, when, how, to build up your talk. Do they need more data – if so, what? Should they feel differently – how? Should they take action – when? After deciding your objective, choose some mental prompts which consist of your key words. You could build on the previous speaker's comments or briefly summarise what has been said and add your own views.

EXTEMPORANEOUS SPEAKING

Whereas the impromptu speech has to be made with only a couple of minutes of preparation time, there is a similar form of presentation that is called extemporaneous. This is the art of giving a carefully prepared presentation, but making it sound spontaneous by not using notes. Winston Churchill had brought this technique to a fine art. Apparently one of his colleagues is reported to have heard him on numerous occasions practising his impromptu speeches. 'Honourable Members, I did not intend to say this in the House today . . .!'

For most people, it is extremely difficult to memorise a presentation and then to present it, word for word, extemporaneously. There is a constant danger that if you forget one key word, you will lose your ideas, continuity and spontaneity. One way of overcoming this is to learn to speak from ideas alone – from personal experience and knowledge; then the words will come. If you have a good memory, you can memorise the general outline of the presentation, and a few key words on cards should suffice.

Both the impromptu and extemporaneous presentation should include the other vital ingredients to make them a success: enthusiasm and vitality! PMA is especially important on these occasions.

THE LECTURE

The lecture is a popular method of presentation when large groups of people are involved. The presenter or lecturer is imparting information to her audience. There are certain **advantages** in this method of presentation:

- It is an effective way to present material to large groups.
- It can be used to give the outline or background to a very broad subject, of which the details can be given later by other presentation techniques; for example, in

Other Types of Presentation

small group presentations, discussion groups, using supporting material such as reports and papers.

- It can allow large quantities of material to be presented very quickly.

The **disadvantages** are:

- The audience is not involved. If the presenter does not actively attempt to keep the attention level high, then the audience will lose interest. This is made more difficult because of the volume of information which is being presented.
- There is no feedback. The presenter does not know if she is on the right track, or if the audience is taking in the information being put across.

Here are some hints on preparing the lecture. Prepare as you would for any other presentation.

Know your objectives and those of your audience.

Research your audience and your material.

Have a clear structure to your lecture.

Hook audience attention in the opening and emphasise the key points. Tell them what's in it for them.

Check that your verbals and non-verbals match up. Be enthusiastic and positive.

Be aware of the non-verbal communication of your audience. Be prepared to change the pace if, for example, the audience is getting restless or looks bored.

Maintain interest by including humour, anecdotes, examples, as appropriate.

Summarise frequently.

End on a positive note.

Decide which visual aids are most suitable for the size of audience. A lectern is useful for holding notes – practise the smooth management of the latter.

Have a full dress rehearsal, checking equipment, microphone, lighting. If someone is working your audio visuals, check cues with them.

The word 'lecture' conjures up unhappy memories for many people: hours of boredom listening to experts extol the virtues of their particular theory; the university professor reading his latest paper. It doesn't have to be that way. More than any other type of presentation, the lecture to large audiences takes on the aura of a theatrical event: everything should be slightly more exaggerated, the voice, the gestures. Keep it lively – and keep them interested!

PRESENTING A PAPER

This can present certain problems. Is it a presentation or a reading? You will, of course, be required to follow the normal practices of the organising body, but otherwise, I suggest that you tackle this as you would a business presentation.

Firstly, prepare a presentation. Use your preparation checklist for this. Follow the advice on structure, delivery, visual aids. Gather together all the material on your subject. Go through every document, reference, item of correspondence. Retrace the whole project from inception to completion and check all your facts. This will refresh your memory. You will be surprised at how much detail you had forgotten.

When you have completed the presentation, have a rehearsal. When you are happy with the finished result, start on your paper. You have now done most of the work, so writing the paper should be relatively easy. You now

Other Types of Presentation

have a shape in your mind, you have revised the relevant materials, and you have prepared what you are going to say, in conversational style. Your preparation, enthusiasm, and knowledge will be evident to your audience and they will respond by sitting up and taking notice.

THE TECHNICAL PRESENTATION

Technical professionals are often let down by poor presentation skills. They may be highly talented and knowledgeable in technical areas, but are often bypassed for promotion by less efficient colleagues who present well and project what management sees as the right image. It is important for technical professionals to be exposed to other groups. High visibility can also be extremely useful in gathering support for technical ideas.

As well as adhering to the general rules for presentation preparation, the technical specialist needs to take particular care when deciding what level of detail is required by the audience. All too often the technical presentation can sink in a morass of technical detail and jargon.

Examine your audience carefully. For example, you may be asked to give an informative talk to the local Rotary Club on the latest information technology. Although your audience will consist of intelligent business people, don't assume that they know even the basics about the subject. Simple words that are common in the world of computing and communications are not always understood by the general public. Another audience may be a gathering of technical staff. You may be part of a group presentation, where you provide the technical expertise. Here you can go into more detail.

In every instance, technical presentations should be delivered at a level of understanding that is comfortable for your listeners. If you talk above or below their level of understanding, they will stop listening.

Very often, the technical presentation will include a product demonstration. Give the demonstration rehearsal as much time and effort as the rest of the presentation. Check everything and thoroughly review your 'What if . . .' list. When giving the presentation to non-technical groups:

- Briefly explain any technical jargon which you will use.
- Encourage questions throughout the presentation. This will enable the audience to clarify any points that are unclear.
- Keep the information short and punchy. Give the minimum of detail to meet your objectives.
- Allow a reasonable length of time for questions at the end.

COMPETITIVE PRESENTATIONS

Professional services are offered by a growing number of consultants, many of whom are women starting up in business for the first time. We live in competitive times and the nature of the consultancy business means that time is money. The simple format of:

>Preparation
>Professionalism
>Persistency

will help you formulate your approach.

Preparation

This stage should be very familiar to you by now. Time and effort spent beforehand is the rule. Whilst it is not

Other Types of Presentation

realistic to expect to win them all, careful planning will provide a better strike rate.

There are growing numbers of professional competitors in all the market sectors, eager for business. Very often initial meetings with clients and the process that follows are conducted in parallel with others. This first meeting is important to demonstrate professional competence. If this initial contact is not favourable, then you may not get the opportunity for further discussion.

Clients themselves are increasingly demanding. They do not assume that the first person to walk through the door is fine to appoint. Nor do they regard the relationship, once started, as 'for life'. They expect the consultant to understand their business, their market and their problems.

Let's imagine that you, as a consultant, have made an initial appointment to meet a prospective client. Here is a checklist to help you think through your strategy:

- Gather together all the information on the company before the first meeting: information by telephone, company reports, sales literature.

- Know who you will be talking to at the meeting and their position with the company, their role in the decision-making process. Ask if they are speaking with other consultants. Clients are very often quite open about this information.

- Try and define the objectives, i.e. what the client is looking for. At the initial stages this is often difficult to define, but you will have at least a general idea. Look for connections. How might you be able to help? Any recommendations? Are there areas that require clarification?

- Be prepared to take along some of your own work, literature, case histories, success record, which show your professionaliism (often referred to as extrinsic selling).

- Personal presentation; remember you are the company you represent. (See section on dress.)

Professionalism

In demonstrating professionalism, it is important that we distinguish between 'the professional salesman' and the professional who can sell. In most cases, clients are looking for the latter. Creativity and a professional approach are crucial for success. This must be apparent to the client from the beginning or they will not take the matter further.

Show an interest in the company. Ask questions and make it clear that you have done your homework. Use questioning techniques to elicit information, which will help you identify the root problem as quickly as possible. Show a grasp and understanding of the client's actual situation, and in the early stages make a 'pass' at a solution to demonstrate competence. Agree on the next stage, which is likely to be a written proposal from you.

Use a systematic approach. Put as much effort into this stage as you would into a formal presentation. Research and prepare thoroughly. The written proposal should look and read well: use clear language and focus on the client, identifying the present situation, making the proposal and outlining the benefits to client.

After all the discussion, preparation and rehearsal, the presentation must then be made. At the end of the day the client may change the brief, or say, 'I'll think about it.'

Persistency

Success in part goes to those who are persistent, who follow up confidently and who, when successful, maintain a good client relationship.

Other Types of Presentation

HOW TO INTRODUCE ANOTHER SPEAKER

When you can make a well prepared and delivered introduction of another speaker, you assist that person to get off to a good start. A good introduction will put *you* in a good light, as well as the speaker. To organise this kind of presentation use the 'TIPS' formula:

- T Stands for TOPIC. Speak first of the topic, giving the title of the presentation.
- I Stands for IMPORTANCE. Tell the audience what's in it for them, and why they should listen. Sell them on the benefits.
- PS Stands for PRESENT the SPEAKER. Now give the speaker's qualifications. In the final two or three words of your introduction, announce the speaker's name clearly and distinctly.

Consider the following in your delivery:

- Be brief. Do not speak for more than one minute.
- Be conversational; speak just as you would to a friend.
- Remember your PMA! Be enthusiastic. Act as if it is a privilege to introduce this speaker.
- Above all, be warmly sincere.
- Reiterate the guest speaker's name at the end of your introduction.
- Mention only one or two important qualifications of the speaker – relevant to the topic.

VOTES OF THANKS

At some time or other, you may be required to give a vote of thanks to a guest speaker. A vote of thanks is a mark of courtesy, and sincerity is the keynote. Treat this occasion as a mini presentation. It is one of the few presentation occasions where you should not use notes. Make it ACE:

Assessment

Give a genuine assessment of the presenter's performance. Emphasise the positive and helpful aspects of the presentation. For example, 'We listened with great interest to Ms Smith's views on... Personally, I was extremely impressed by the enthusiastic way she outlined... She has paid us the compliment of presenting the benefits in a clear and objective way. The greatest tribute which we can make to her will be through the adoption of her proposals.' 'But perhaps our greatest delight has been in the way in which Ms Smith has succeeded in bringing her somewhat unusual subject to life. She has proved that... need not be a dull topic. She has enlivened our evening with wit and humour as well as some good common sense.'

Close with Enthusiasm

'And so, in thanking Ms Smith for coming along this afternoon, I can only hope that we can welcome her back soon. We wish her every success in the future and a speedy return visit. Thank you, Ms Smith, very much indeed.'

PRESENTATIONS TO FOREIGN GROUPS

More and more presentations are being given to foreign audiences, to whom English is not the first language. Here are some tips on dealing with foreign audiences.

If possible, allow for some tuning-in time, where the listeners can tune in to your voice, your intonation and

Other Types of Presentation

your accent. The registration or coffee time before the presentation is ideal for this purpose. If this is not possible, then allow for a few minutes at the beginning of the presentation – perhaps when you welcome them to the event.

Use short words and sentences. Many foreigners have a higher level of proficiency in the reading of English than they have in the spoken language. To maximise understanding, only put one idea into each sentence. Speak clearly, and give the audience time to digest the information.

As in any presentation, break up your information. Review it in the light of the ability of the listeners to take in the information. Remember these pointers on information:

introduced on a 'quick fix' basis = confusion;
poorly paced = uninteresting;
too much, too soon = information overload.

Avoid technical terms, jargon, slang and clichés, and use active verbs and concrete nouns. Research at a number of institutions in the UK and the USA indicates that approximately 78 per cent of the English language, as it is used in daily life, is composed of active sentence structures. For example, 'We evaluated (active verb) the reaction of the audience' instead of 'Audience reactions were evaluated' (passive verb).

Pace yourself carefully. Pause at the end of each sentence or phrase. Your audience then has time to catch up and digest the information. Remember the earlier tip of pausing before and after important facts and statements.

Always put important information at the end of a sentence and never at the beginning.

11
Survey

This part of the survey is based on the answers to a questionnaire completed by a hundred women in business.

Today, more and more women are having to give presentations. Generally, when asked how they feel about giving them, they will say things like, 'I feel I have to work harder because I'm a woman', or 'I'm the only woman in an all male team – I often think I am not taken seriously.' Rarely will they admit to enjoying giving presentations. This is understandable, as many women don't get feedback, particularly from male colleagues. Although they have a general feeling of 'I think that went down well', or 'that could have been better', this lack of feedback frequently doesn't add to what may already be a low confidence level. Women often take 'no feedback' as being negative.

Women working in traditionally male environments also face difficulties in that their experiences are different from those of men. Women often talk about male cliques and a general feeling of unease when they are presenting to 'groups' of men. Often they feel that they are being judged firstly as a 'woman' and not for what they know, (i.e. stereotyping), even though they may be more knowledgeable about the subject than the males. A feeling of vulnerability is fostered because women in general will show their feelings; for example, they will admit that they are nervous or inexperienced, whereas men generally avoid doing so, particularly in all-male groups. If

Presenting For Women in Business

1. INTRODUCTION
2. QUESTIONNAIRE RESULTS
3. ADVICE FROM WOMEN
4. THE MALE VIEWPOINT
5. SUMMARY

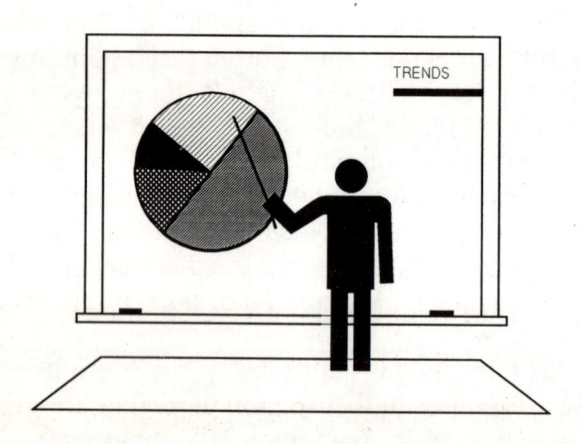

Survey re. women giving presentations

Survey

they are going to say anything about their feelings, it is usually done discreetly – like a male on one of my courses who sidled up to me and whispered in my ear, 'Has anyone ever fainted when doing their presentation?'

It is no wonder that women often feel that men make more confident presenters. They rarely put themselves down or admit to their inadequacies. Also women report having few role models in their own company. Men can gain experience and advice from other male colleagues, and are readily given a pat on the back for a job well done.

OBJECTIVES OF THE QUESTIONNAIRE

To find out:

- what women *feel* about giving presentations. (When presenting to *male audiences*, do they approach the subject in the same way as for women?)
- what *advice* they would give to new women presenters in the light of their own experience.
- the *feedback* they have received from male audiences.
- *role models* whom they feel display the qualities of a good woman presenter.
- results of asking *a hundred men to name the qualities* they look for in a woman presenter.

Are there differences between the male and female presenter, and in the attitudes towards them? Or do women 'perceive' these differences?

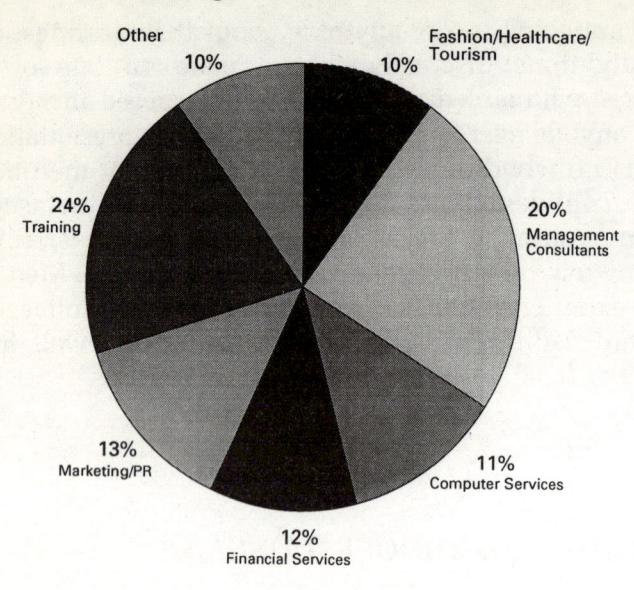

Presenting For Women in Business

- Other: 10%
- Fashion/Healthcare/Tourism: 10%
- Management Consultants: 20%
- Computer Services: 11%
- Financial Services: 12%
- Marketing/PR: 13%
- Training: 24%

Survey Breakdown – 100 women from the following business sectors:

Business Sectors	
Fashion/Healthcare/Tourism	10
Training	24
Financial Services	12
Computer Services	11
Marketing/PR	13
Management Consultants	20
Other (Retail/Legal/Sales/ Pharmaceutical/Textile/Mfg/ Engineering/Transport	10

Respondents by business sector

Survey

[Bar chart showing respondents by responsibility category:
- Personnel: 32
- Training: 33
- Marketing: 29
- PR: 27
- Sales: 9
- Financial Services: 4
- Administration/Secretarial: 4
- Other: 13]

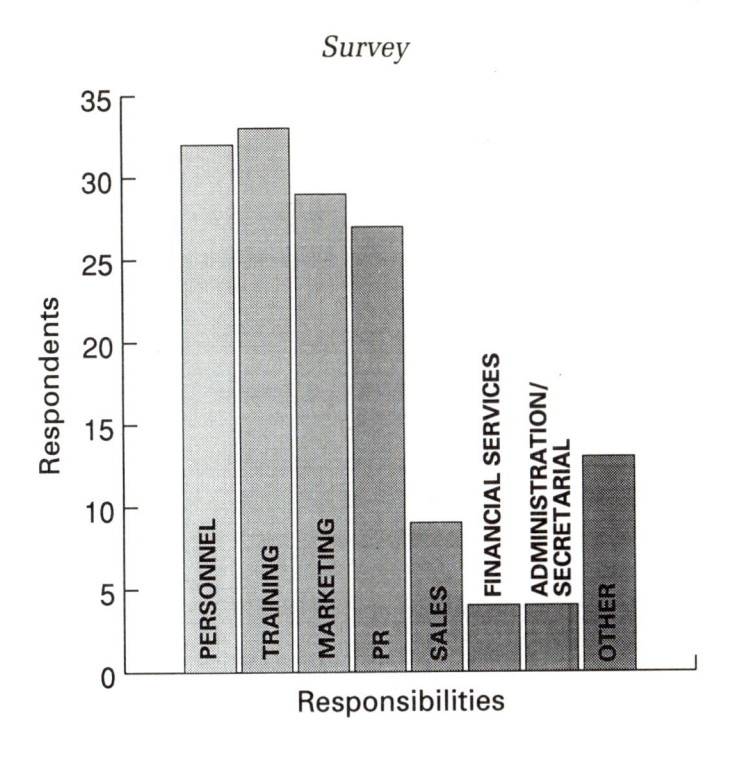

Responsibilities	
Personnel	32
Training	33
Marketing	29
PR	27
Sales	9
Financial Services	4
Admin/Secretarial	4
Other	13

Respondents' responsibilities

QUESTIONNAIRE RESPONSES

Question 1
What are your feelings about giving presentations?

I enjoy giving presentations a) Always
                              b) Sometimes
                              c) Never

Circle the most appropriate answer and make any comments.

Results:
a) Always – 39%   b) Sometimes – 54%   c) Never – 6%
d) Other – 1%

a) Always
Of the 39 per cent of women who responded 'always', a few also made comments and gave reasons for their choice.

Maureen, a partner in the building and construction industry:
'I am continually trying to improve my presentations. I am pushing myself further by working towards giving presentations in schools, encouraging schoolchildren to work in the building and construction industry.'

Christine, a personnel and training consultant:
'The opportunity to enlighten, inform and motivate people to aid their own development or progress projects.'

Susan, an advisor in financial services:
'Passing on my own experience is always enjoyable.'

Maxine, an organisation development consultant:
'While I always look forward to a presentation, it is not without some stage fright and lots of concerns about getting all aspects to click.'

Survey

'I enjoy giving presentations'

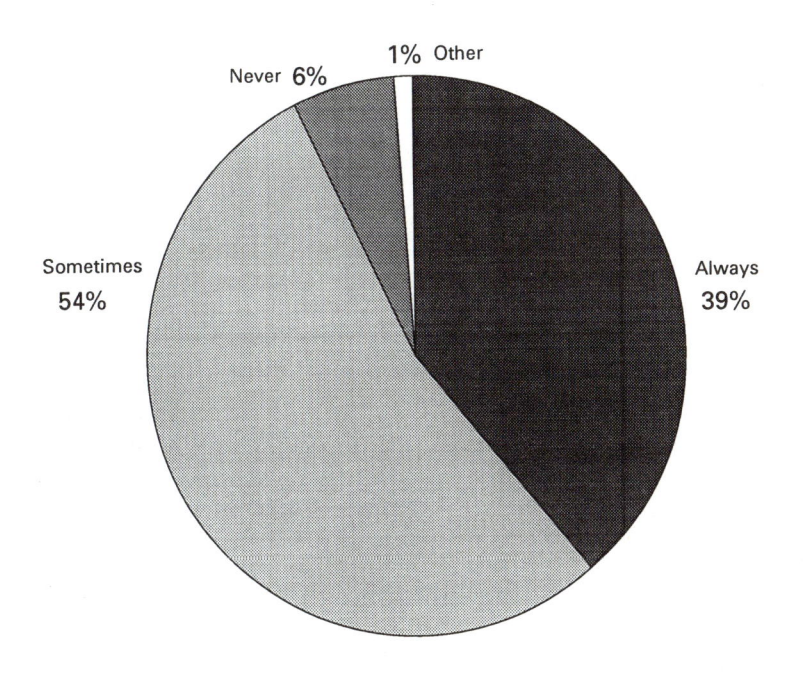

1% Other
Never 6%
Sometimes 54%
Always 39%

Feelings about giving presentations

Ann, transport services:
'I used to loathe it. Usually these days I am giving out a message which is important to me and I know that I know my subject.'

Mary, a training officer in the retail sector:
'It wasn't always this way. For years I hated giving presentations and training. That was with my previous company. I now enjoy my work, it's a good company with good products. I really look forward to standing up and telling new recruits all about it. I'm told my enthusiasm rubs off on them! (They are all female!)'

Jane, account executive, PR company:
'I enjoy meeting and presenting to potential clients. I must be doing something right as my success rate is very good.'

Four of the respondents qualified the always response by adding either 'almost' 'mostly' or 'nearly'.

b) Sometimes

Only two of the 54 per cent of women who responded 'sometimes' made comments. Both said that the difference between choosing to answer b) and not a), was the lack of preparation time. Shortage of time added to their stress levels. One said she often didn't have time to rehearse; the other felt that because she knew she had spent insufficient time in preparation, her performance on the day was not a true reflection of her capabilities.

c) Never

In all, 6 per cent of women answered with a resounding 'never' and they added these comments.

Trudy, business manager in the fashion industry:
'"Enjoy" is too strongly expressed. I *never mind* giving a presentation and people can easily twist my arm to volunteer to give one.'

Survey

Maureen, personnel manager, central Government:
'A vicious circle – I never have enough practice to be good at it and hence I don't improve! I lack confidence in addressing people when I'm in the position of imparting specialist knowledge (new to the audience). The sense of 'power' does give some confidence, but I still feel I might make a hash of it!'

Julie, staff officer, education:
'I'm always extremely nervous and 'over-prepared' because I can't rely on thinking/talking on my feet. I'm afraid of being asked questions I won't be able to answer!'

Caroline, financial services director:
'I feel scared/self conscious/anxious and so on'

Anne, supervisor, plastics industry:
'Am worried about knowing my subject adequately enough to be able to give comprehensive answers to questions which will arise. As for my appearance – am I coming across in a confident manner or do I appear unsure of myself?'

Margaret, business development manager, agricultural chemicals:
'Lack of confidence to think on my feet. Presentations where I have read a prepared script are usually well received, but on less formal/internal presentations a formal script is not appropriate.'

Ashley, personnel manager in manufacturing, added a new category: d) 'I'm beginning to'

Question 2 was about the Audience.

a) As a woman presenter, do you ever give presentations to predominantly male audiences?

Please answer Yes or No.

Presenting For Women in Business

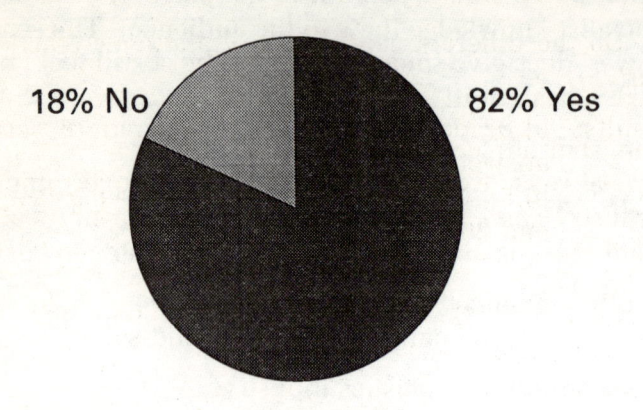

a) *'I give presentations to predominantly male audiences'*

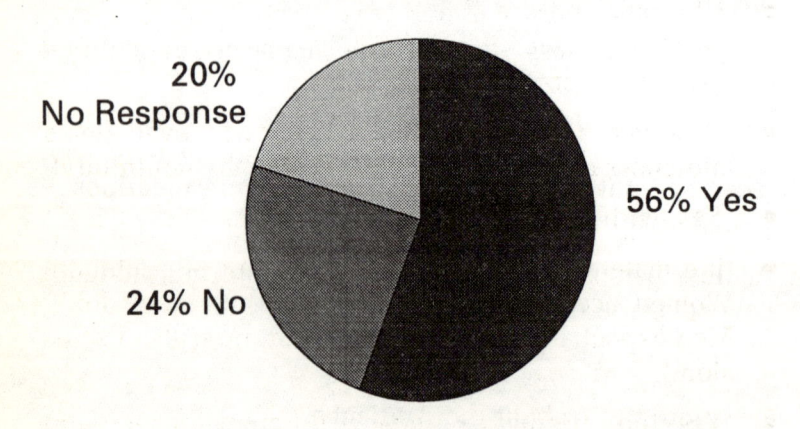

- 82% Yes
- 18% No

b) *'I treat audiences of different genders differently'*

- 56% Yes
- 24% No
- 20% No Response

Survey

If you answer Yes please give your feelings about this. For example, do you approach the topic in the same way as you would for a group consisting of women?

b) Do the different genders affect audience reaction to you?

Results: a) 82 per cent answered YES and 18 per cent answered NO to this
b) 56 per cent answered YES, 24 per cent NO, and 20 per cent gave no answer.

a) Not all of the women stated how they felt about presenting to male audiences, but here are the comments of those who did.

- 'The seniority of individuals rather than their sex will affect me more. However, in most cases the most senior people tend also to be male!'
- 'I become more nervous when presenting to senior people and feel less confident and will therefore spend far more time in preparation.'
- 'However, I often feel that I can "win over" male audiences easier than female by using my femininity!'
- 'Yes, with confidence and a smile.'
- 'If a male audience, I double check my presentation. Women accept the occasional mishap – men don't. Men expect a short and to the point, no frills, discussion.'
- 'Yes, the information I give is different for men and women.' (Fashion consultant)
- 'I probably would – I have never presented to a mostly female group. I am more nervous of male questioners than female.'

Presenting For Women in Business

- 'There is a tendency to win men over with more explanation than I feel would be the case with women. Men appear more cynical.'
- 'I have generally felt in the past that it has been harder work to present to a group of men – I find them more aggressive and direct than women, which automatically puts me on the defensive.'
- 'Depends on the topic – if professional, yes – if political, possibly not.'
- 'I would be more informal with a group of women, more inclined to show my personality.'
- 'I approach it in much the same way. Maybe I use my eyes differently. Body language might also be different.'
- 'I relax more when presenting to women, adopt a less formal approach.'
- 'I expect men to be less sympathetic than women. I try to communicate to men on a purely professional level, whereas with women, I can empathise.'
- 'I find it more frightening speaking to an all-male audience.'
- 'I find it easier to "connect" with an all-female group.'
- 'Have to establish my credibility as early as possible. Women are more willing to give you a chance. Also, less jokes, as men may take it the wrong way!'
- 'I feel that a male audience often has lower expectations of my contribution than the female group, particularly when the subject is technical.'
- 'More serious and formal with an all-male group.'
- 'I try not to feel inferior. Hence the reason for trying to improve myself all the time.'

Survey

- 'I feel that I can be more theatrical with the presentation, telling more stories/jokes, being more of a ham and more assertive than with a female audience. Women in general seem more intimately responsive.'

- 'More conscious of needing to gain their respect in the very early stages of the presentation. Ability to respond to negative vibes and involve potential disrupters!' Facts impress.

- 'I have to present technical information and present regularly alongside male colleagues. I find that if they make a mistake, it's overlooked. If I do, then it's because I'm a women (implying that I don't understand, am not technically competent, etc.)'

- 'I am very aware of some men looking for inconsistencies, so I make sure I do my research. Mostly, men are courteous.'

- 'Feel intimidated sometimes, but that depends on the audience – for example, age, seniority, attitude to material and *me*.'

- 'In most cases men may be more sympathetic/more willing to listen because of the novelty factor. Women would take me more seriously.'

- 'I make sure that I come across as a total expert initially, so that my gender is not seen as a problem. Is this the nanny syndrome I wonder? Well, it seems to work with the men. For women I don't feel the need to show I know what I'm talking about, it's easier to be more informal and at one with the audience – more adult-to-adult.'

- 'I deliberately foster intimacy with a female group. With a male group I keep to the point of the presentation.'

- 'I feel positive about it – I'm aware there are often things I have to do to 'gain their ear'/convince them I have something worth saying – otherwise okay.'
- 'I try to make more preparation for difficult and typically biased questions.'
- 'I feel more confident in front of predominantly male audiences. I make more jokes because I feel more relaxed.'

Twelve respondents who answered 'yes' to having presented to predominantly male audiences said that they did not consider the gender issue. Their approach would be based mainly on: the formality of the occasion, their own objectives, and the seniority, knowledge and needs of the audience.

One wit replied: 'I'm tempted to say that I use simpler words – but that is just my sense of humour. Seriously, the approach would really depend on the topic.'

There were no comments from the 18 per cent of women who answered 'no' to this question.

b) Of those who replied 'yes' to the question 'Do the different genders affect audience reaction to you?', many of the replies were very similar to those of question a).

Again, a representative sample:
- 'With predominantly male audiences you get the "pack" mentality – they stick together and sometimes behave like little boys, with naughty remarks and trying to catch you out.'
- 'I certainly find that credibility is more of an issue with all-male groups, whereas women seem to accept me as someone who wants to help.'

Survey

- 'I run seminars for many clients. I have to face prejudice on the grounds of being (i) female (ii) younger than the audience and (iii) an "outsider", i.e. consultant.'

- 'Men are more competitive, but are happy to take advice based on experience.'

- 'I feel it is important not to be seen as an "empty head" or just a "skirt"; so I would use more technical jargon.'

- 'Mistakes made by men may not be noticed as readily as mistakes made by women. But once your audience realises you have something to say, you will be respected.'

- 'As a young, relatively inexperienced personnel manager, I have to work hard to be taken seriously.'

- 'When talking about technical matters/problems, I have to be adequately prepared, i.e. research the subject, be able to give details of past and present trends and come up with some positive ideas.'

- 'I try to indicate early on that even if my experiences as a female are different from theirs, I too have acquired the success factors they crave – so I go for credibility.'

- 'I find that when working with a male colleague, their credibility is automatic unless they don't perform well, whilst my credibility has to be established.'

- 'It seems to be a male pastime to make life that little bit more difficult for women presenters.'

- 'A group of men will tend to regard you as a representative of all womankind and treat you accordingly (and judge you accordingly also), if you are the only woman present.'

- 'My way of winning men over is to get them on my side by showing my knowledge of my subject in relation to their needs. Once they understand I do know my subject, they are more receptive and willing to help. It is useless relying on looks alone.'

- 'I occasionally have to "show the stripes on my arm" to establish authority – particularly with some older, less well educated men, and with the "young bloods" who tend to show off.'

- 'Once credibility is established, I generally find male groups *more* supportive.'

- 'I feel I get more attention *because* I am a woman in some cases, e.g. sales force/national accounts presentations.'

- 'I think women are slightly more sympathetic towards the female presenter. In my experience, women are more likely to give you a pat on the back, if it's good, or a shoulder to cry on, if otherwise!'

- 'I do feel that I have to work harder to establish credibility. I sometimes feel I could be the token woman speaker, so enjoy rising to the challenge to "sock it to 'em". I rely on my enthusiasm and bounce as the main tools in my armoury.'

Question 3
Advice to new women presenters.
The next question asked for advice to new women presenters. Name the three most important aspects you would urge them to consider:

Results: the three most popular areas of advice:

Preparation
Dress/Appearance
Voice

Survey

Key Areas of Importance

1. Preparation

2. Dress/Appearance

3. Voice

Advice to new women presenters

Question 4

Have you ever had feedback about presentations that you have given? Answer Yes or No.
If yes, please give examples.

Results:
82 per cent of the respondents answered Yes and 18 per cent No. Of the 82 per cent who had received feedback, most reported the feedback was positive and constructive.

Many women reported receiving positive feedback, even when they felt nervous about their own performance. Here are some of their comments:

- 'My scripted presentations always had good feedback. Less formal presentations to senior management – I was advised to be more confident and less nervous. Not such good feedback on presentations I made at short notice.'

- 'Enthusiastic response from audience during and after presentation. On second visit I was given a "glowing" introduction. Of course, I then had to live up to my introduction! That was threatening.'

- 'I've had lots of feedback – from the man who said, "I was really surprised when *you* stood up and took over, I thought you were the administrator" to "How can you have gained enough experience at your age, dear, to be able to talk about sales management?" Maybe he was trying to compliment me?'

- 'Recently I got a "Well done, dear", which I think was in sympathy because I was so obviously nervous.'

- 'Capable and informed. Awesome (I think this may be a joke, I'm still trying to deal with it.)' 'Powerful – indeed too powerful for her own good' (indirect feedback from male).'

Survey

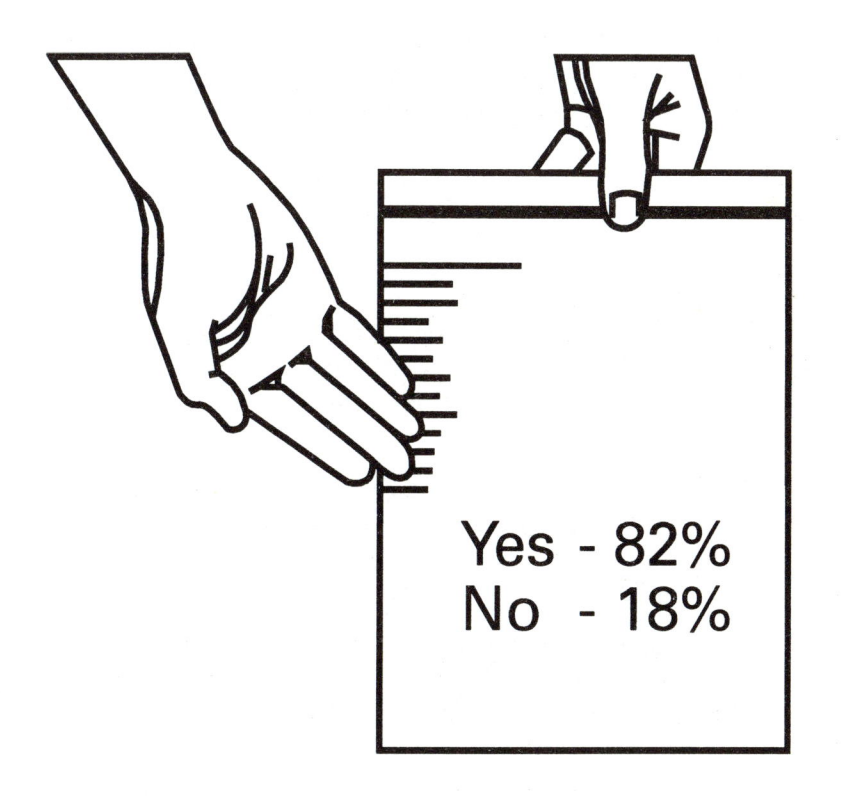

Yes - 82%
No - 18%

'I have received feedback'

Presenting For Women in Business

- 'Challenging, fun, surprising, disconcerting, a relief, opened up a whole new perspective on life and a way of communication. As well as the "You could have..."'
- 'Good. The content and presentation came over as professional, you knew what you were talking about.' 'You are objective and straight – no hidden messages – we know where you stand.'
- 'Courteous and grateful responses – but this has always seemed to be more a response to the message than to the messenger.'

When you give a good presentation you are *remembered*. One woman summed it up in her response:

- 'Branch and area managers invite me to speak because other managers have recommended me.'

Many women stressed the importance of gaining feedback. Here is how one woman (a toastmistress) replied:

- 'I've been a member of ITC (International Training in Communication). It was one of the best moves of my life and has generated enormous rewards in learning, confidence and friendships. Outside ITC I've found people terribly reluctant ever to give you constructive (or even destructive) feedback. People join ITC to get feedback, that's why this is so valuable.'

Most of the constructive feedback from men encouraged women to be more assertive and confident.
One woman even said:

- 'The training manager for whom I worked used to video our presentations so that we could learn to avoid distracting/irritating mannerisms. Video is *the* most powerful feedback mechanism.'

Survey

Question 5
Role Model
Can you name a woman whom you admire as a presenter and give reasons for your choice?

Ten women did not answer this question. Two made the comment that the question made them realise how few there are! Twenty women named colleagues or former colleagues. One woman replied: 'This is a ludicrous question. Why should I admire one person more than another? A good presenter presents themselves and their material well!'

Another woman named her mother, a lecturer. She says, 'My mother is very confident, assertive and has great presentation skills.' And adds, 'Pity it is difficult to take advice from one's own mother!'

The most popular choice was Kate Adie. This is perhaps not surprising, as she has been very much in the news.

Here are the choices. They show a compilation of the general qualities, with specific comments in quotes below.

Kate Adie *TV broadcaster, reporter*	Clear, concise, confident, open to questions, prepares well; articulate, poised, calm in stressful situations, e.g. Gulf crisis. Very professional. 'I heard her speak at a lunch. She was clear, interesting and humorous.'
Rt. Hon. **Margaret Thatcher** *former Prime Minister*	She is always taken seriously. Appears to listen – an important aspect of selling. She learned to use TV cameras to her advantage, although she voted against it in Parliament.

Presenting For Women in Business

	Never loses her cool! Singleminded, interesting, commands attention 'Best use of autocue at conference that I have ever seen.'
Anita Roddick *Chairman,* *The Body Shop*	Knows all the answers.
Julia Somerville *Newsreader,* *ITN News*	Good voice, emphasises main points. Good control. Instils feeling of belief in the listener.
Sue Lawley *TV presenter*	Honesty, humanity, humour. Well prepared, friendly, confident. Unruffled by unexpected questions. Good use of voice – doesn't patronise. Always look businesslike, but feminine. Manages to introduce a little lightness when interviewing.
Anna Ford *TV newsreader*	Quiet self-confidence, clear voice, steady gaze. Attractive, without being flashy. Sounds as if she knows what she's talking about.
Brenda Dean *General Secretary,* *SOGAT*	'One of the few women in high places who comes over sounding sensible, and not – "I am a high-powered, successful woman in business who didn't get where I am today by being soft." '
Joan Ruddock *MP*	Calm, confident, non-ingratiating.

Survey

Jill Dando *TV newsreader*	Efficient, but pleasant face. Nice suits. Relaxed and competent.
Mavis Nicholson *Broadcaster,* *TV presenter*	Good preparation, right pitch of voice. Excellent listener, has a genuine interest in subject. Doesn't flaunt her gender – an all-round professional
Angela Rippon *Broadcaster,* *TV presenter*	Professional, well prepared, versatile. Well groomed with attention to detail. Positive body language.
Judith Chalmers *Broadcaster,* *TV presenter*	Behaves naturally. Treats the audience with respect – yet she's like an old friend.
Rt. Hon. **Lynda Chalker** *MP*	Professional and confident.
Judith Hann *Presenter of* *'Tomorrows World'*	Smart dresser, pleasant manner. Clear speaker, knowledgeable. 'Presents a complicated subject in a simple interesting manner.'
Moira Stuart *BBC newsreader*	Well prepared, firm and agreeable.
Baroness **Barbara Castle** *Euro MP*	Use of anecdotes. Confident, looks good. Coherent and logical.
Rt. Hon **Shirley Williams** *former MP*	Marvellous knowledge. Speaks with conviction, strong opinions. Articulate and able to think on her feet

Presenting For Women in Business

	and to look at different viewpoints. N.B. Nothing at all to do with appearance – she's a good presenter because you *listen* to her.
Joanna Foster *Chair, Equal Opportunities Commission*	Clear and concise. Commitment and enthusiasm 'Recognised as an authority.'
Mrs Mary Baker *Freeman of the City of London*	Talks with ease and confidence. Comes over as an energetic person. 'She has achieved a great deal in her own right, and makes speeches that say something of importance.'
Detta O'Cathain *Managing Director, Barbican Centre*	Clear voice, pleasant personality. Doesn't talk down to her audience.
Eleanor McDonald *Founder, Women in Management*	Honest, direct but homely. Articulate. 'What she says is based on her own experience (sometimes hard won experience at that) – a pioneer of her day!'
Selina Scott *TV presenter*	Professional, talks with authority. Knows her subject. 'Well educated, perhaps a little too clever for some men, especially in the media world.'
Yve Newbold *Company Secretary, Hanson plc.*	Supremely confident, relaxed. Not patronising.

Survey

Edwina Currie *MP*	Confident, relaxed. 'She listens well to questions – not surprisingly!'
Ruby Wax *Entertainer*	'She's a delight to watch for me.'

Presenting For Women in Business

'Just to break the ice, can you tell me – are you wearing stockings or tights?'

(What one woman experienced when addressing a group of personnel managers.)

12
The Secrets of Effective Women Presenters

> *EVE POLLARD, Editor, Sunday Mirror*
>
> I think women need the same skills for public speaking as men do:
>
> be clear, concise, with humour if possible.

> *JANET SUZMAN, Actress*
>
> These are the three things which come to mind:
>
> know your subject;
>
> find a lower register in your voice;
>
> be yourself.

Presenting For Women in Business

The secrets of effective women presenters

JANCIS ROBINSON, Wine writer, TV presenter

My advice is to speak with confidence, lots of projection and no apologetic mutterings or breathy flutterings. Even if you're saying something you may feel doubtful about, the fact that you have the microphone or whatever adds credence to it.

However creatively you normally dress, choose something slightly neater (if not necessarily more conservative) for public appearances. This especially applies to hair: flyaway hairstyles can be very distracting to look at.

Many people, myself included, experience drowsiness immediately before an event as a symptom of nerves. Taking a series of deep breaths is very good for waking one up and steadying the nerves.

The Secret of Effective Women Presenters

KATHERINE WHITEHORN, Columnist, The Observer

My advice to new presenters:

Clarity is for any presenter or communicator, male or female, the number one requirement and I think different types of people tend to muddy the waters in different ways. On the whole, women are slightly more inclined to do it by unclarity of sentences or by whispering or muttering or confusing hand signals and so forth. They say, 'I mean', 'well, really', 'it's a case of . . .', 'isn't it?' and things like that, where they actually want to come out with a clear statement.

Even if you're quaking inside (and you probably are), come across as if you know what you are saying and are sufficiently confident to say it with some humour and not too dogmatically. The public doesn't always appreciate that the person who bangs the drum and says, 'I am right and I will brook no disagreement of any kind' is actually the person who is deeply unsure inside. The more confident you are, the more you can say, 'I think the way I would approach it is . . .' rather than 'Now listen here, you must do this'.

The third is a slightly more diffuse category – it consists of not spoiling your chances of coming across well by things which are entirely irrelevant. This includes incorrect dress – whether too aggressive or too humdrum; it includes things like not making sure thaat your microphone is working, that the relevant cameraman is focused upon you, that you can acutally read the teleprompter, that you can see your notes; and determination to make sure that you have understood the brief and are dealing with it in the way in which you were asked to do.

CLARE FRANCIS, Author

I would advise women presenters to:

be ruthlessly self-critical.
Make tapes of your voice – eradicate irritating habits.
Examine video tapes of your performance and be prepared to learn from them.

be confident without being abrasive (whatever anyone says, no one likes abrasive females!)
Develop your own viewpoint/approach.
Do *tons* of homework.

Listen to what others are saying in an interview situation. This is true for all presenters whatever their sex, but is still the most frequently forgotten.

JOANNA LUMLEY, Actress

If you are reading autocue or a speech, make sure you've said it *aloud* at least twice. Check *all* pronunciations. Don't rush and be sure you know what you're talking about. Remember that you're only speaking to a few people – even if it's broadcast to millions.

Dress simply and effectively, have tidy hair and good make-up, then forget what you look like. Don't fidget with rings or bracelets. Avoid bright red or royal blue because of strobing. Clean your teeth before transmission or recording.

Be friendly. Be determined to enjoy yourself. People are only people.

The Secret of Effective Women Presenters

VALERIE GROVE, Writer, interviewer, Sunday Times

Three main aspects to consider:

warmth and enthusiasm;

intelligence; and

mastery of the subject.

JOAN BAKEWELL, TV Presenter/interviewer

Clarity: to be heard;

dispassionate presentation: to be believed;

fluency: to be enjoyed.

Julia Somerville, Sue Lawley and Anna Ford display these qualities.

ANN WIDDECOMBE, MP

Stop worrying about the fact that you are a woman. It is usually quite irrelevant to the case you have to present. If you are engaged in debate, do not be too rude about people who will speak *after* you.

Forget image – self will out.

JANE ASHER, Actress, writer

Choose an outfit you feel *secure* in – no possibility of slip showing, shoulder straps falling, etc. If anything, slightly underdress rather than risk going over the top. If it's a particularly nerve-wracking occasion, try not to wear something you've never worn before.

Try to speak from the heart – easier said than done, I know. Be truthful and simple, don't try to be clever. *Don't* try to be funny, unless you're sure it'll come off! If you can, speak from memory or by improvising but, if necessary, have a few key words on a card. It seems much more genuine if you don't read it all, word for word.

Everyone gets nervous – it would be unnatural if you didn't, but remember that your audience *wants* to hear you. They're not against you.

I have a little trick for calming my fright before speaking. I imagine that I've had some really terrible news, something quite devastating (in my case, something to do with my family). Then I remind myself that it's not true – only pretend – or even continue my fantasy to the point where someone comes to tell me everything's all right after all. Then, having to make a speech seems so totally unimportant and trivial compared with the awful scenario I have just pictured that I feel ashamed to be nervous and grateful that the important things in life are OK. I can swan through the speech, knowing how relatively silly it all is!

The Secret of Effective Women Presenters

ANNE HOOPER, Writer, broadcaster, LBC

As a beginner, you are going to make mistakes. As a broadcaster, they are public ones, so . . . don't be hard on yourself. The mistakes sound worse to you than to the listening public, who are in fact fascinated by anything that sounds personal.

So that you can sound as smooth as possible, write down any phrases and phone numbers you need to have at your fingertips. Begin by writing, i.e. preparing, introductions, etc.

Admit mistakes when you make them and make no bones about repeating something correctly. This sounds better than flustered confusion.

EMMA NICHOLSON, MP

Good deportment: standing, sitting, walking. This gives confidence to you and your audience. They need reassurance on your confidence level; someone too nervous creates nervous tension in the viewer or interviewer. Good deportment also gives good breath control, vital for effective speaking.

Appropriate clothes and make-up are important. If applying for one style of job, don't dress or present yourself as right for another. High heels don't work on the farm, nor dungarees in the House of Commons.

A smiling face – cheerfulness is catching; they'll want to take you on in preference to someone gloomy.

Presenting For Women in Business

ROSABETH MOSS KANTER, Professor, Harvard University

The first and most fundamental skill is to be an expert and to know your subject well. People are more interested in substance than in style, and style is something that can be cultivated later. But if you have nothing to say, that certainly shows. For any group that is not yet well accepted in the workplace and has to prove that people who are members of that particular group belong and have credibility, there is no substitute for the certainty of clear knowledge.

The second important skill is self-confidence – which shows in the ability to claim all the space on a stage or at the head of a conference table; to move around the room; to recover quickly from mistakes and even make a joke out of them; and to be flexible enough to bring in new material spontaneously or to make changes on the spot.

The third key skill is to empathise with the audience. It is important that their needs be met and that the emotional state of the audience be kept first and foremost in the presenter's mind. It is up to the presenter to relax a tense audience with a joke, to reassure people that difficult subjects will be handled well, and to treat members of the audience as individuals who are potential friends and supporters.

The Secret of Effective Women Presenters

ANGELA RUMBOLD, MP

I think presentation skills are most important for professional images. It is important for women to learn to communicate and make public speeches and of course the best advice I can give on that is to practise constantly . . .

If you are making any kind of public speech, the most important thing to remember is that first of all you should know your subject. Secondly, I think it is important to feel comfortable in your clothes and to know that you look good. Thirdly, of course, as I said, the most effective way of overcoming nerves is to gain confidence by more and more practice.

It may be of some assistance to you to know that even those of us who earn our living principally by making public speeches do still, from time to time, get attacks of nerves. That does not necessarily mean that we cannot make good speeches!

ANN WINTERTON, MP

Speak clearly (if no one can hear you, their interest will disappear within seconds) and be sure of your facts and the message you want to leave with your audience.

Be suitably and comfortably dressed. It will give you confidence if you know you look your best.

Be well briefed on your role, e.g. how long you have to speak, subject matter etc. Take every opportunity to speak in public to perfect the art.

EDWINA CURRIE, MP

Use of voice:
you need to learn how to use the microphone, or if there is no mike, how to ensure everyone present can hear. It helps if they can see you – so stand up. Don't mumble and keep your head up.

Knowledge and message:
if they can hear you, then they will listen. Tell them something they don't know. Use simple language. Work out in advance what 'message' they should take home, and hammer away at it.

Appearance:
dress for your audience. They should say to themselves, 'Looks OK' when you stand up, but should not be distracted by your appearance after that.

ROSIE BARNES, MP

Know your subject well enough to be able to speak without notes. Use only headlines. However, have notes to hand as a safety net, in case you dry up.

Look your best and feel comfortable. This is essential for confidence, which is the key to good presentation.

Know your audience so you hit the right level. It is fatal to speak above or below the level of those listening.

The Secret of Effective Women Presenters

MARGARET EWING, MP

Know in advance what your opening and closing remarks will be. Opening remarks are very important – all of us get nervous about starting, so confidence is critical. Closing remarks are important because they leave a final impression; what is said in between is often lost!

Take time to look smart. Confidence in your own appearance is important. The audience may forget your words of wisdom, but they won't forget an untidy hairdo, laddered tights or dirty shoes.

Always remember that the vast majority of people could not/would not go up front and speak. Therefore *you* are different; use your difference to advantage. Be natural, be firm, but never forget what it has taken to be there – you believe in your views and have worked to express them!

LLIN GOLDING, MP

If you can, include a joke.

Know your audience.

Do not ramble on and on; know where to stop.

MARGARET BECKETT, MP

Always stand up. Many women have quite soft voices and it is easier for people to hear them, and also to be able to supplement what they can hear by the movement of lips, if they can actually see your face. In addition, far more people than is generally realised are at least a little deaf and most are not prepared to admit it.

Don't apologise for your supposed inadequacies. Probably nobody will notice them if you don't point them out. Just remember, everyone else is just as nervous as you are and trying hard not to show it. Experience and practice nevertheless will always help.

Try to say what you mean as clearly and simply as you can.

Dr MARJORIE MOWLAM, MP

Personal appearance – sadly, people judge what you say by how you look.

Be human – not too aggressive.

Present a clear, concise argument.

I think that after-dinner speaking is harder for women, because the listeners frequently expect a *risqué* joke and innuendos and women simply can't behave in that way.

The Secret of Effective Women Presenters

Mrs Y.M. NEWBOLD, Co. Secretary, Hanson plc.

With regard to presentations, which I have to do quite frequently, I do not now rely on cards or notes of what I am going to say. There is a very good method used by the Front Bench in the House of Commons whereby the whole script is prepared in advance. The speaker needs a lot of practice, ideally with video, to be able to read the script whilst looking up at the audience for quite long periods. The full script of what one is going to say reduces nerves to manageable proportions (I do lots of deep breathing beforehand anyway). It is essential to practise making the words sound as if you are saying them conversationally and the script itself must be typed in large script with certain words highlighted. This is an excellent method where the subject matter is quite technical.

I rely on personal anecdotes quite a lot, because I find these break up an otherwise dry subject. I often start off with a dramatic sentence, but there is the danger with this that the rest of the speech can be a letdown. I try to finish on a summary and a dramatic note or a quotation or a funny line. I generally let the audience know a few minutes before the end that I am ending in another few minutes. I say things like 'In closing, let me say . . .' or 'Finally, I would like to say . . .' or 'And one last point . . .'.

With dress, I try to aim for formal, but bright, to stand out from the rest of the audience. A blouse in a bolder colour than one would normally wear is good. I generally go for a jacket of some kind, because it adds gravitas. Flat heels look dreadful to an audience so I always wear high heels. I try to look at the audience in a sweep that is like my Flymo doing the lawn, a sort of left to right and back again arc, starting at the front and working on down the audience.

Presenting For Women in Business

> *ANNE ROBINSON, Presenter,*
> *'Points of View', BBC1*
>
> I consider the three most important aspects of good presentation to be:
>
> intelligence, clarity and wit.

13
What Men Look for in Women Presenters

THE MALE VIEW

A hundred businessmen were asked what quality they look for in a good woman presenter.

The responses varied, but the most frequently mentioned came under the general headings of preparation, confidence and appearance. Here are some of their comments:

Self-Confidence

- 'Must be self-assured, so that the audience is immediately made to feel that this is going to be a worthwhile presentation. First impressions conveying this message are critical. This may be particularly difficult in male-dominated subject areas but, in my experience, women presenters can overcome this problem through self-assurance.'
- 'Natural movement, open and relaxed. Inspires confidence in the listeners – which in turn gives *you* more confidence.'
- 'Do not apologise or be coy. This devalues the presenter and the subject.'
- 'Speak up, with confidence and authority'.

Presenting For Women in Business

What men look for in women presenters

What Men Look For in Women Presenters

- 'Don't be afraid to be yourself. Your audience is there because they want to hear what you have to say. Just act natural.'

- 'Authority – you must have an air of experience.'

Appearance

- 'Dress appropriately. If you are underdressed, in particular, it may affect your confidence and make you feel ill at ease. It may also lead your audience to devalue the message, if they feel that you have not made any effort.'

- 'Men invariably don't start to listen until they have had a good look! The sooner you can get them to stop looking, the sooner they start listening.'

- 'I like to see a woman presenter who is smart and professional – I look for the same qualities in her material and delivery.'

- 'Sadly necessary – no one wants to look at an unmade bed!'

- 'Mostly a horror story. Messy hair; lack of care with face; wrinkles, bulges and bits in clothes; wrong style of dress for the job, accessories.'

- 'My major problem with women is non-verbal rather than structural. They often just *look* wrong.'

- 'I make no fundamental distinction between male and female presenters. However, it is assumed that dressing in good taste is desirable if only to appear credible.'

One male said: 'I've attended a lot of seminars in my time and I have to admit that boobs viewed via a low-cut dress, coupled with an above-the-knee dress slit to the thigh, would have helped me through a lot of them!' (For obvious reasons I will not identify him.)

Other comments:

- 'Know your subject – you positively *must* know what you are talking about – and in addition have knowledge *around* your subject.'
- 'Take the time to research and prepare properly what is to be presented. Leave yourself enough time to achieve this and thus avoid the all too frequent, last-minute rush (the photocopier is down again!) and the attendant mistakes, inaccuracies and missing material.'
- 'You must be thoroughly briefed on the subject matter and be able to answer in-depth questions.'
- 'Talk to your audience and watch their reactions. Be prepared to alter *how* you put your points across. Establish a communications link with the audience. By looking at them and gauging their reactions you will know whether you are succeeding.'
- 'Ability to decode message so that it is understandable is essential.'

When asked to name a woman presenter who possessed the qualities which he admired most, Tim Lindsay, joint managing director of Bartle Bogle & Heggarty, had no hesitation in naming a colleague who exhibited sincerity, clarity and humour. He adds that these are exactly the same qualities that one needs to look for in a male presenter.

In fact, 10 per cent of the men questioned named a colleague or ex-colleague. Most were vague about this question, but the most popular women presenters were Kate Adie, Anna Ford and Moira Stuart.

15 per cent of the men said that they could not differentiate between the qualities required for male and female presenters, as summed up by one male:

'I started out trying to think of particular female problems in presenting and quickly came to the conclusion that a Presenter is a Presenter is a Presenter! My answers apply equally to male and female. I do not see any divide in today's world or indeed within my own company!'

GODFREY SMITH, Times Columnist

The qualities required for women presenters are exactly the same as for men.

Accuracy: without which no other quality is any use.

Clarity: easy to say, terribly hard to pull off (with it goes that other cardinal rule – brevity).

Humanity: it's not much good telling it like it is and sounding like a metronome or a dalek. Here women have a built-in advantage.

SIR ROBIN DAY, TV Broadcaster, interviewer

Intelligence: including political awareness

Looks: but neither distractingly glamorous, nor distractingly plain

Personality: including e.g. authority, presence, charm, wit and guts

---

CLEMENT FREUD, Writer, broadcaster, caterer

Advice: not to be embarrassing.

Presenting For Women in Business

PETER MORGAN, Director General, Institute of Directors

Forget that you're a female, apart from being well presented and professionally turned out.

Humour always helps.

Tell 'em what you will tell them. Tell 'em – three points. Tell 'em what you've told them.

VISCOUNT WEYMOUTH, Director, Longleat Enterprises

Grasp of subject; interest falls away if this is suspect.

Interesting literate presentation including humour.

Attractive personality, so that we *like* you.

PETER JAY, Writer, broadcaster, economic & business editor, BBC

Intelligence: viewers can spot a 'dummy' very fast.

Knowledge of subject: you cannot interview intelligently if you don't know what you are talking about.

Ability to communicate: this simply means fluency and vocabulary. There are *no* important TV techniques; just be your own bright, intelligent and communicative self.

What Men Look For in Women Presenters

SIR VIVIAN FUCHS FRS,
(Leader Trans – Antarctic Expedition)

It has not occurred to me that women require any more or different advice than an inexperienced male speaker.

SIR JOHN HARVEY-JONES, MBE,
Chairman Parallax Ent., ex-ICI,
Writer, broadcaster

I look for confidence (even though the presenter may not feel it), humour and originality.

I prefer a presentation from notes rather than a real speech; it makes me believe the presenter knows her stuff.

I like to have eye contact with the presenter since it eases the interpretation of her phrases and words.

SIR PETER PARKER, Chairman, Mitsubishi Electronics UK

It doesn't matter a damn what gender. The paramount skill is to be yourself. If a woman, then stay that way in performance – don't think you have to be macho (or dress that way for that matter).

Be of good 'humour' – grave matters seem often to be even graver when women presenters go po-faced; be human – I don't mean joke.

Presenting For Women in Business

SIR PETER USTINOV, Actor, dramatist, film director

Try to avoid making remarks intended to be amusing which, however, inspire no reaction, and which lead to the speaker saying, 'No, but seriously', before going on. Better far to pretend the unfunny remark was serious in the first place, which, in a way, it was.

It is essential to give the impression your words are felt rather than learnt; not as easy as it seems. Most politicians stumble at this hurdle, for the simple reason that their texts were written by someone else.

Don't be too conscious of the fact that you are a woman. Just forget it, and act 'natural'. They'll probably guess you're a woman in any case.

MILES KINGTON, Humorist, columnist, The Independent

I am so unused to the ways of business that I do not know what a 'presenter in business' is. I know what a TV presenter is: do people in business behave like TV presenters? No wonder British business is in a bad way. But I can give you some advice for women speakers in public:

Speak as low as possible.

Tell dirty jokes which all the men present fail to understand, but all the women think are hilarious.

Say fairly frequently 'For the men present, I think I had better explain what that means . . .'

He adds 'I am not saying this would work. But I would like to be there when it was tried out!'. (So would we!)

What Men Look For in Women Presenters

Many of the men, when asked to name a woman presenter whom they admire, were very coy. Not so Godfrey Smith, *Sunday Times* columnist; he printed his reply to the question in his column, extolling the virtues of Kate Adie. Then he sent me his reply – YES – THE INCOMPARABLE KATE ADIE. It is an excellent choice, shared by many of the men and women who were asked the question; talk about shouting it from the rooftops!

One man went even further. Earlier we had some advice from Jancis Robinson on appearance (see page 175), stressing that 'however creatively you normally dress, choose something slightly neater (if not necessarily more convervative) for public appearances.' Sounds good, Jancis. Now here is what a TV reviewer for the *Today* newspaper had to say about her programme, 'Matters of Taste':

'Jancis Robinson could talk about the inside of a ping pong ball for half an hour and still make her subject sound sexy. And at the risk of sounding really sexist, I would just like to say that it wouldn't matter what she talked about – just listening to and looking at her is a feast in itself. Now I've discoverd Jancis Robinson, I shall race round Sainsbury's with renewed vigour.

Last night she was Channel-hopping between Salford – home of Vimto, the Eccles cake and the modern vegetarian movement (no, I didn't know that either) – and its twin French town Narbonne, home of horsemeat and frogs' legs. She looked like something out of *The Country Diary of An Edwardian Lady*, and she glided along leafy French river banks in straw hat, dirndl skirt and flowing white jacket. At any minute I expected her to throw away her hat, tear off her oversized, orange-framed glasses (the kind that look gross on Christopher Biggins but appear so elegant on Jancis) and make wild, passionate love to a Narbonne butcher.

She has that delicious, prim look of a maidenly schoolteacher, but you know there are uncontrollable passions – albeit about food and drink – stirring underneath. She presents her subject informatively and engagingly without being patronising.

Fascinating gastronomic crumbs of information were dropped from Jancis's table. And when she started rummaging through Salford Polytechnic lecturer Patrick's fridge, I could hardly contain my excitement. Jancis, you can chill my radishes any day.'

Help, we can't win – is this what happens when we dress conservatively?

SUMMARY

It is obvious that male and female presenters have many more similarities in their personalities, goals and behaviour than differences.

The main differences appear to be centred around the fact that men are surrounded by 'male' role models. They can observe at first hand the benefits of developing competent management skills (or otherwise). They are encouraged to promote themselves and, in many companies, are more likely to be offered training.

In the questionnaire, only one in five women could name a colleague as role model. Many more named women in the media, government or organisations where women have high profiles.

Most of the feedback given to this sample of presenters was positive. It is interesting to note how many of the men urged women to be more assertive and confident. Again, this is based on their own experience; these are the qualities that men strive for themselves. Generally, the men seemed to admire the qualities which the women themselves rated highly in the questionnaire, i.e. being well prepared and knowledgeable, with a professional appearance and manner. Or, as one male put it, 'Look good, sound good, and sock it to them!'

What Men Look For in Women Presenters

It would appear that there *should* be no basic differences between the sexes, if we are striving for the same goals. We share the same destination, but clearly many women feel that they are 'on the road less travelled.' The difference may lie in the different 'experiences' encountered on the journey. Also encouraging was the fact that so many of the men admired women who could 'be themselves' or, as several said, 'act naturally', i.e. as a woman and not trying to act like a man.

When identifying the qualities of a good female presenter, the women responded with lots more heart (feeling) responses, than did the men. For example, they used more adjectives like 'warm', 'agreeable', 'friendly', 'helpful'. Men tended to respond with head (fact) words. For example, 'knowledge', 'technical detail', 'intelligence', 'control'. This does not mean that women don't consider these areas, quite the reverse; what it means is that women express the information differently.

Finally, here is some feedback which one woman was given after her presentation:

'I enjoyed your presentation. You were really well prepared and knew your stuff. It was nice to have a woman presenter for a change, it adds a *different* dimension – a softer approach.' He then quickly added 'I'm not saying it was *better* than a male presenter, just different. But it was a refreshing change . . .'

Vive la différence!

14
The Future

> 'We don't discriminate positively at Channel 4, we just choose the best men for the jobs, and quite a lot of the time they turn out to be women.'
>
> Liz Forgan
> Head of Programmes, Channel 4

CHANGE IN ATTITUDE

Many people believe that exposure to today's working women is playing a large part in shifting the attitudes of corporate leaders, who are mainly white, middle class, middle-aged and quite often titled. But there's an economic point as well; there's no doubt that many of Britain's most influential chairmen recognise that more has to be done to attract women, as business and industry are becoming more competitive.

Cosmopolitan magazine undertook a survey of Britain's 25 biggest companies, as identified in the November 1990 edition of *Business* magazine. Their aim: to investigate male attitudes to promoting women to senior positions within the company. They spoke to the chairmen of the various companies concerned and asked their views.

Dalgety chairman, Sir Peter Carey, told *Cosmopolitan* of his desire to see more women in senior management. He also observed that in many (male-dominated) companies 'there exists a subconscious bias, a feeling that a woman is not actually going to do the job as well as a man.' Carey has made few concessions at Dalgety. He has no women on his board, is vague about how many women he has in management positions, operates no career break scheme, does not believe in offering any female training and development courses and devolves responsibility for policy to Dalgety's individual companies. On a personal note, he believes having children is 'the ultimate privilege' and refers to AGM questions about getting a woman on the board as 'militantly feminist'.

But it is not just men who are having problems. Hanson company secretary Yve Newbold (who gave us some good advice in Chapter 12) came face to face with the dilemma when one of her own staff became pregnant and put off her decision whether or not to return to work until after she'd had the baby. 'When you face it yourself, all the theoretical stuff goes and you're brought back to basics with a crunch,' says Newbold. 'Do you train somebody else? Do you regret you didn't employ a man in the first place? When it strikes you first-hand, heck, it's hard.'

Society's ability to accept career interruptions without prejudice is a long way off. To promote women to senior positions, particularly in male dominated professions, involves a major shift in attitude. But there may be a glimmer of hope on the horizon, as *Cosmopolitan* discovered when they interviewed Sir Allen Sheppard, Chairman of Grand Metropolitan. He sounded somewhat embarrassed about not having a woman on the board at Grand Met: 'There are nine of us, all men in boring grey suits, white and middle class. It's the classic stereotype. I do see there is a danger of men sitting down and discussing the specific needs of women, which is crazy. I'm currently pursuing one particular woman, in the right sense of that word, I hasten to add!'

Lady Howe is Chair of the Women's Economic Development Initiative, a group aimed at making industry more aware of the changing economic role of women, for its umbrella group, Business in the Community. She agrees that it's the heads of companies who should lead

The Future

in this area. She expresses enthusiasm about how female employee policy is evolving and predicts 'considerable change' over the next five to ten years.

Many companies are acting now, for example Tesco, where Sir Ian MacLauren instigated research to find out why only two out of 387 of his store managers were women. As a result, more women have been encouraged to take up senior positions. At ICI the number of women moving into middle and senior management has trebled in the last five years. Last year British Gas recruited 48 female gas fitters – another first – while Sainsbury's have completely revised their management structure to accommodate women.

> **'I believe it is incredibly important for women to support other women, so that in time success and achievement are not remarkable by gender.'**
>
> *Brenda Dean,*
> *General Secretary, SOGAT*

SUGGESTIONS FOR ACTION:

- Take the advice of Sir Peter Ustinov and many other men questioned in the survey – act natural (i.e. like a woman).
- Voice your opinions and actively support the many groups involved in progressing the role of women.
- Take every opportunity to encourage and support other women.
- Grasp every opportunity to update skills, seek training, build confidence and gain experience.
- Educate the men, by demonstrating your competence and by competing on equal terms (but enjoy the special differences).

Presenting For Women in Business

- Volunteer to make presentations and ask for feedback.
- Cultivate your sense of humour. How about applying Miles Kington's advice at your next presentation?

TRAINING

'Fear of the unknown is the real enemy. I believe some presentation skills are innate (a love of performance, a desire to be the centre of attention, an ability to think clearly and speak articulately), but much can be taught. Training! If people are trained to present effectively, the fear vanishes!'

(*Woman manager*)

For information on presentation skills training for business men and women contact:

> Communication Works Ltd
> 47 Marloes Road
> Kensington
> London W8 6LA
> Telephone: 071–938–2025
> Fax: 071–938–2241

We specialise in individual and small group training either in-house or at our distinctive training centre. Communication Works and its associated companies offer a range of services, including Business Ethics consultancy and training; Strategic Communications advice and Crime Management services.

Bibliography

'Are we among equals?', *Director*, February, 1990

Bell, Gordon, *Speaking and Business Presentations*, Heinemann Professional Publishing, 1987

Carmichael, Sheena, and Drummond, John, *Good Business: A Guide to Business Ethics*, Century Hutchinson Business Books, 1989

Currie, Edwina *et al.*, *What Women Want*, Sidgwick & Jackson Ltd, 1990

Dean, Brenda, 'Women at work', *Women and Training News*, October 1990

Dix, Carol, *A Chance for the Top*, Transworld Publishers Ltd, 1990

'Dorothy Sarnoff' Profile, *PR Week*, June 1986

Fast, Julius, *Body Language*, Pan Books, 1972

'Focus', *The Independent*, December 1990

Gelb, Michael, *Present Yourself*, Aurum Press Ltd, 1988

'Industry's leading ladies', *Works Management,* October 1990

'Issues and opinions – diffusing the demographic time-bomb', *Women in Management Journal*, July 1990

Janner, Greville, *Janner on Presentation*, Business Books, 1984

Jay, Anthony, *Effective Presentation*, British Institute of Management, 1970

'The Labour Market', *Personnel Today,* October 1989

Leeds, Dorothy, *Power Speak,* Piatkus Books, 1989

Morse, Stephen, *The Practical Approach to Business Presentations,* Management Update Ltd, 1980

'The Young Ones', *Personnel Today,* October 1989

Index

Accent, 63
Adie, Kate, 190, 195
Agenda, 28, 66
Alternative
  approach, 26–7, 42
  sources of labour, 2–3
Appearance, 77, 85–91,
  189–90, 196
Asher, Jane, 178
Aspel, Michael, 69
Assumptions, 7–8, 65
Attention
  curve, 34
  hook, 31–2, 41
Attitude, positive, 66–7, 73
Attitudes, changing, 1, 4–6,
  11–12, 199
Audience
  needs, 21, 29, 42, 58, 67,
    99, 117
  profile, 21–2
  size, 23–4
Audio-visual aids, 53
Autocue, 177

Baker, Mrs Mary, 170
Bakewell, Joan, 177
Barnes, Rosie, 9, 182
Bartle Bogle & Heggarty, 190

Basinger, Kim, 106
Beckett, Margaret, MP, 184
Behaviour, types of, 5
Benefits, sell the, 65
Body
  language, 74–95
  of presentation, 32, 39, 48
Brainstorming, 28, 45
Breathing, 70, 82, 84, 175
Bromley, Professor D. B., 93
Burton, Richard, 69

Cards, use of, 48–50
Carroll, Lewis, 10
Castle, Barbara, Baroness,
  169
Chalker, Rt. Hon. Lynda, 169
Chalmers, Judith, 169
Churchill, Winston, 136
Clichés, 145
Client, presentation, 92
Close
  of presentation, 32, 121,
    144
  types of, 42, 48
Communication, 13, 63–74
Competitive, presentations,
  140–2

Confidence, 147, 157, 160, 166–8, 180, 184, 187, 196
Conviction, 18
Cosmopolitan, magazine, survey, 199–200
Critique, presentation, 133–4
Currie, Edwina, MP, 8, 182

Dando, Jill, 169
Day, Sir Robin, 191
Dean, Brenda, 168, 201
Demographics, effect of, 1–15
Display, board, 108
Dress, choice of, 85–91, 94–6

Editing, 46–7
Einstein, Dr Albert, 117
Enthusiasm, 67, 73, 85, 136, 144
Equal Opportunities Commission, EOC, 2–3
Ethics, business, 47, 202
Ewing, Margaret, MP, 183
Examples, use of, 40, 137
Extemporaneous speaking, 135–6
Eye contact, 71–2, 78, 193

Facial expression, 78–9
Fatigue, effects of, 19
Feedback, 91–3, 164–6
Female role models, 5, 13, 149
Flip chart, 105–6
Ford, Anna, 168
Forgan, Liz, 199
Foreign groups, presentations to, 144–5
Foster, Joanna, 170
Francis, Clare, 176

Freud, Clement, 191
Fuchs, Sir Vivian, 193

Gestures, 80, 95
Golding, Llin, MP, 183
Group presentation, 27–8
Grove, Valerie, 177

Handouts, 29
Hann, Judith, 169
Harvey-Jones, Sir John, 193
Hook, uses of the, 35–6
Hooper, Anne, 179
Howe, Lady, 200
Humour, uses of, 40, 192–3, 202

Impromptu speaking, 135–6
Introducing another speaker, 143
Introduction, *see under* Structure

Jay, Peter, 192
Johnson, Dr, 56

Kanter, Rosabeth Moss, 32, 180
Keller, Helen, 10
King, Billie-Jean, 72
Kington, Miles, 194

Language, use of, 145
Lawley, Sue, 168
Lecture presentation, 136–7
Listening skills, 19–20
Lumley, Joanna, 176

Magnetic board, 108
McDonald, Eleanor, 170
Morgan, Peter, 192

Index

Mowlam, Dr Marjorie, 184

Nerves, 81–5, 155, 157, 164
Newbold, Yve Mrs, 185, 200
Nicholson, Emma, MP, 179
Nicholson, Mavis, 169
Notes, use of, 48–56

Objection, handling, 123, 126
Objectives, 19–22, 30
O'Cathain, Detta, 170
Opening impact, 32–3, 36–9
Optimism, future, 10–15
Overhead projector, 101
Overlays, transparency, 100–4

Parker, Sir Peter, 193
Pollard, Eve, 173
Posture, 77, 80
Preparation and planning, 19–29
  see also Set up and rehearsal
Preparation checklist, 30

Questions,
  audience checklist, 129–30
  fielding of, 122–3
Quotations, use of, 36

Rippon, Angela, 169
Robinson, Anne, 186
Robinson, Jancis, 174

Roddick, Anita, 168
Room layouts, 24–5
Ruddock, Joan, MP, 168
Rumbold, Angela, MP, 181

Scott, Selina, 170
Set up and rehearsal, 131–2
Somerville, Julia, 168
Smith, Godfrey, 191, 195
Structure of the presentation, 31–43
Stuart, Moira, 169
Suzman, Janet, 173

Technical presentation, 139
Thanks, votes of, 143–4
Thatcher, Rt. Hon. Margaret, 167
Timing, 56–8

Ustinov, Sir Peter, 194, 201

Visual aids, types and uses of, 97–116
Voice, use of, 67–71

Wax, Ruby, 171
Weymouth, Viscount, 192
Whitehorn, Katherine, 175
Widdecombe, Ann, MP, 177
Williams, Rt. Hon. Shirley, 169
Winterton, Ann, MP, 181

The Mercury titles on the pages that follow may also be of interest.

All Mercury books are available from booksellers or, in case of difficulty, from:

Mercury Books
Gold Arrow Publications Ltd
862 Garratt Lane
London SW17 ONB

Further details and the complete catalogue of Mercury business books are also available from the above address.

Peter Amis and Jackie Head
THE SALESMAN'S HANDBOOK
THE SALESWOMAN'S HANDBOOK

The Saleman's Handbook and *The Salewoman's Handbook* are substantially the same book – a complete guide to selling for men and women alike.

The books are designed to be used and carried around as an important part of the basic selling toolkit. They contain detailed practical guidance on:

- researching & planning the call pattern
- getting to the real decision-makers
- the opening position
- step by step negotiation
- closing the sale

The Authors: *Peter Amis is a freelance training consultant specialising in sales and customer service training. With a number of years' experience in sales and marketing he left industry to join a training organisation where he ultimately became managing director before becoming a consultant.*

Jackie Head is a freelance training consultant, her specialist areas being selling, customer care and management development.

'A complete mobile sales trainer.' *Sales and Marketing Management*

ISBN 1–85251–064–1	£14.95
ISBN 1–85251–110–9	£14.95

Janet Cameron
THE COMPETITIVE WOMAN

Only men cling to the creaking myth that a woman has to be a bitch to be boss! But women do have to use all their feminine wiles to compete in today's business world and overtake male rivals in the climb to the top. That's the conclusion of successful business woman Janet Cameron in *The Competitive Woman*, based on her own experiences and 'go-it-alone' approach.

Janet Cameron highlights the four essential characteristics a woman needs to get on in business – pride, confidence, optimism and a thick skin! She draws on her own experiences running a highly successful office supplies business and provides case histories of other women who have made it to the top of their particular field through a variety of leadership styles.

The Author: *Janet Cameron started out in business as a sales representative for a printing firm working from a small flat in South London and is now a highly successful businesswoman in her own right, having set up her own office supplies company in 1973.*

'Covers everything from business functions to boardroom battles, from hostilities to harassment – with insights, anecdotes and survival tips from an insider.'
Cosmopolitan

ISBN 1–85252–086–8   £6.99 (paperback)